# LEADING
## TECHNOLOGY
# DRIVEN
## TRANSFORMATION

**Four steps to take control of technology driven change in the financial services industry**

## Esther De La Cruz

First published by OMNE Publishing in 2016

National Library of Australia Cataloguing-in-Publication entry

Creator: De la Cruz, Esther, author.

Title: Leading technology driven transformation : four steps to take control of technology driven change in the financial services industry / Esther De La Cruz.

ISBN: 9780994415509 (pbk.)

Notes: Includes index.

Subjects: Technological innovations.
Leadership.
Financial services industry.

Dewey Number: 658.4063

Editing by Grammarfactory
Photography by Deanna Gerlach
Cover design by Designerbility
Layout by OMNE Author Solutions

Printed by OMNE Publishing www.omne.com.au

*'A person who never made a mistake, never tried anything new.'*

*— Albert Einstein*

# *CONTENTS*

**Introduction: The challenges of change**     **1**

The call for change leadership     6

The challenges of leadership     9

4 steps to become a great leader of change     11

    Step 1: Clarity     13

    Step 2: Context     14

    Step 3: Collaboration     14

    Step 4: Control     15

The benefits     16

Who am I?     18

It's time to become a leader of change     21

**Step 1: Clarity**     **23**

Gathering the business requirements     30

The existing technology landscape     39

Build a relationship with reference sites     40

Research key areas     41

Compile your learnings     44

Key takeaways     48

**Step 2: Context**     **51**

Defining and prioritising the key business drivers for the change     53

The value of sharing your key business drivers for the change     57

Create a vision for your technology innovation journey     60

Establish a roadmap for the change     64

Key takeaways     67

**Step 3: Collaborate**     **69**

Collaborating with the business     77

    1. Understand what other business divisions want to achieve     79

    2. Manage the human element of change     81

    3. Communicate early     82

    4. Communicate transparently     84

    5. Communicate often     85

    6. Be conscious of your body language     87

    7. Share the 'why' behind your vision     89

    8. Develop a communications plan     91

Collaborating with your team     95

    1. Choose the right resources     96

    2. Recruit diversity     101

    4. Sharing your priorities     103

    5. Involve your team in your vision     104

    6. Help team members develop relationships     105

Key takeaways     106

**Step 4: Control**     **107**

Risk identification     112

Revisiting risk     116

Managing risks     119

Risk management learnings from Intel IT     122

Key takeaways     124

**Conclusion: Become a great leader of change**     **127**

**Acknowledgements**     **133**

**About the author**     **137**

## Introduction
# The challenges of change

'Change leadership is going to be the big
challenge of the future, and the fact that
almost nobody is really good at it is — well, it's
obviously a big deal.'

— John Kotter

Change is challenging, unpredictable and present in every industry. And nowhere is change more apparent than in the financial services industry.

The financial services industry is the largest contributor in the services sector to the Australian economy, equally to the mining industry generating 9.3 per cent of total gross value added in the year ending June 2015 and leaving behind construction and manufacturing.[1]

However, that doesn't mean that the industry is without its challenges, with the 2015 IBSA Environment Scan outlining the significant changes facing the financial services industry. These changes can be grouped into four main categories:[2]

1. Policy and regulation changes.
2. Technology transformation.
3. Changing customer needs and expectations.
4. Social investment and climate change.

Let's start by considering policy and regulation changes.

---

1    Austrade, "Why Australia", *Benchmark Report 2016*

2    IBSA, "Predicting change- skills for the future", *Environment scan 2015*

Following the 2008 Global Financial Crisis, the financial services industry has had to work hard at regaining consumers' trust, creating transparency in the way they earn their profits and demonstrating the value they can add. This is demonstrated by recent regulatory changes, including additional reporting requirements, changes to fee structures and increased transparency towards consumers.

Many of these legislative requirements are taking effect immediately and require organisation-wide technology changes, which can initially create inefficiencies, take time to implement and require a significant number of resources.

Regarding technology transformation, there are a number of areas that are having an increasing impact on the financial services industry.

First, the industry is able to collect more customer data than ever before, which allows organisations to get to know their customers better and improve their products and services accordingly. Second, as cybercrime increases, so too do security concerns for these organisations. Finally, the smart phone has become the number one device used by most consumers and business leaders, meaning the rapid innovation and release of new applications for smart phones requires organisations to continually reinvent what they can offer the consumer. This is not just in the release of new and innovative applications, but also through the information that is provided or accessible via these applications.

While this transformation opens up many new opportunities for financial services organisations, it is also rife with challenges and complexity. The most prominent of these is the large number of complex heritage systems present in most of these organisations that do not easily interface with new technology. The way these systems have been integrated (or not) over the years creates huge challenges for continuing innovation. As a result, when considering a new technology solution an organisation will often focus on addressing an issue or pain point rather than innovation and opportunity. This then results in Band-Aid solution after Band-Aid solution, which makes the situation regarding heritage systems even worse.

The third change facing the financial services industry is the change in customer needs and expectations. While the steady flow of funds into superannuation, the growing wealth of Australia's ageing population and emerging markets tapping into Australian investment opportunities will ensure that there is continued demand for financial products and services, there are still challenges when it comes to meeting needs and expectations.

Today's consumers want to be more efficient at engaging with their financial service providers. They are looking for easy-to-access, user-friendly and informative solutions that help them feel empowered and make informed decisions about their financial needs. If they are purchasing a financial service or product, they also want to understand the cost up front. However, customer confidence is low following the government lifting the bonnet and shining a very bright spotlight on the financial advice and financial planning professions. Profits in the industry may have suffered due to this lower level of consumer trust.

The fourth change in the financial services landscape is the increased interest in corporate responsibility. This responsibility comprises the concerns of giving back to the community via social investments and integrating information on climate risk into products and services. While this change is the least likely to trigger technology innovation, it is a critical part of the overall change agenda.

With this changing landscape, it has never been more exciting or more challenging to be a senior leader in the financial services industry.

All of these changes will require some level of technology innovation. It is also likely that most of these changes will be individually addressed with a plan of technology and business transformation to meet the new requirements. Consequently, technology transformation is going to be more present in years to come than ever before.

As a result, the industry needs to get better at these technology implementations. We need to become more efficient, manage our resources more effectively, achieve more benefits and ensure we hang on to great, knowledgeable staff in the process.

The key to achieving this is change leadership.

## THE CALL FOR CHANGE LEADERSHIP

When it comes to implementing changes within an organisation, most organisations refer to 'change management'. In today's business landscape, I believe what we truly need is 'change leadership'.

Dr John Kotter, the founder of Kotter International and creator of the award-winning 8-Step Process for Leading Change argues that change management focuses on the tools, processes and structures that keep the change under control, manage or reduce disruptions to the change, and keep the change within budget.

Meanwhile, change leadership focuses on the vision and strategies that fuel large-scale transformation. Kotter says change leadership is, 'putting an engine on the whole change process, and making it go faster, smarter and more efficiently'. Change leadership makes sure the change happens more efficiently and empowers people from around the organisation to help make it happen.

Change leadership is focused on making sure people understand why the changes are being introduced to the business. Leadership can provide clarity to the broader organisation regarding the need to make these changes in order to achieve business objectives. Leadership can also create alliances of advocates for the change, and these advocates can assist with making the change happen and bringing others along on the journey.

Further, leadership is crucial to creating an open and transparent dialogue about the risks and the challenges associated with the change, which will need to be addressed in order to minimise business disruption and ensure that the changes are embedded in such a way that meet or even exceed business objectives.

This doesn't mean that change management is unnecessary. Rather, the two concepts complement each other. Change management can complement change leadership by taking care of the day-to-day engagement of stakeholders, detailed communications and organising required briefing and training sessions. Change management also can bring to light valuable information that the leader of the change can find useful when embedding the change, including the viewpoints of stakeholders across different impacted business areas and potential change risks.

Similarly, Kotter says that both change management and change leadership have a role to play, but it is important to know when it is needed to switch from one to the other.

In an article on Forbes,[4] John Kotter and his colleague Mike Evans discuss the different indicators that demonstrate when change leadership is required. These include the number of people in your organisation who will need to do something different as a result of the change, how high the stakes are for the change, and whether you need to bring in more expertise to manage the change. To this list I would also add the size of the investment in the change as well as what the change is expected to achieve in relation to the business strategy.

Unfortunately, even when it comes to these large-scale changes, there is very little evidence of change leadership in the financial services industry today. While more and more organisations are seeing the value in hiring change managers to help *control* the change and keep business disruptions to a minimum, very few are looking for professionals who can *lead* the change.

Instead, leaders either tend to stay on the sideline waiting for the technology changes to be implemented or they take a military approach to leadership. Neither of these leadership styles has been proven to be very successful during times of change.

Leaders who stay more on the sideline usually only get involved when things don't go to plan or when the risk of business disruption arises, making them reactive rather than proactive. When roadblocks arise, these leaders tend to analyse the technology aspects of the solution in great detail to move the project forward.

The end result is that important decisions are swayed by circumstances and technology rather than the original intent behind the change, which runs the risk of the new technology solution moving away from the business strategy and vision. Meanwhile, the consequences of military-style leadership are that talented team members stop bringing their ideas to the table, lose their enthusiasm and stop putting thought or effort into their work. I've seen very capable people lose the care factor because they don't need to think anymore.

## THE CHALLENGES OF LEADERSHIP

While a lack of effective change leadership is a significant problem, it's not surprising that there's a lack of this leadership in the financial services industry. Leading an organisation through this changing landscape – whether you are leading the organisation itself or leading one or more technology implementations – is not for the faint hearted.

No longer are you just trying to achieve your business division's goals and objectives, you are trying to stay afloat amid the broader changes in the industry. You are no longer challenged by the changes *you* are trying to create, but more so by the changes that others are creating around you.

You could compare it to being a primary school teacher. A primary school teacher's role is to create basic language skills and a basic understanding of mathematics and geography. At this stage of their lives, children also need to learn social skills and morals. However, it is more challenging than ever before for children to learn these skills with the world around them changing at a faster pace.

With the evolution of social media, smart devices and family demographics, learning styles, behaviour and social rules have all shifted from what they were just ten years ago. This leaves teachers with the challenge of not only teaching children basic academic skills, but of keeping up with technology, new family dimensions and the new ways in which children interact with the world around them.

Similarly, leaders in successful businesses are faced with the basics of running their businesses – developing and delivering products and services, customer communication, financial management and more – while being mindful of the changing marketplace, new competitors and getting the best out of a changing demographic of employees. It's no wonder that more and more leaders find themselves wondering why their roles as leaders seem to get harder every day.

# 4 STEPS TO BECOME A GREAT LEADER OF CHANGE

As with all areas in life, self-reflection is the key to gaining clarity on your strengths and weaknesses as a leader. If you are still reading this book, you are probably already past the denial stage. You have come to realise that you could use some help in managing the massive levels of change that are ruling your professional world at the moment.

You are probably also uncomfortably aware that the sheer volume of change that you have to deal with is not going anywhere. In fact, it seems to be growing at a faster and faster rate. The good thing is that there is a system you can follow that will not only help you manage this change, but *lead* this change. Before I share the four-step program that will put you back in control of large technology changes in your business, I would like to challenge you to reflect on your own leadership style and experience.

- Do you consider yourself to be open and transparent? Do you think others in the business think of you as being open and transparent?

- Do you consider yourself to be authentic? Do you share your thoughts and fears? Are you true to who you are as an individual in your role as a leader?

- Do you take on a strategic role in the changes you manage? Do you delegate most operational tasks so you can focus on the broader vision for the change?

- Do you feel that you are courageous in your role as a leader and call things as you see them?

- Are you adaptive to change and do you easily respond to changes caused by the market, your customers and your competitors?

- Do you think you are doing enough as a leader to ensure that the technology transformations you lead will achieve the best possible outcomes for the business?

If you answered most of these questions with a 'no', that's a sign that you're either stuck in your functional specialty or you're focusing on change management rather than change leadership. Fortunately, there is a solution – four practical steps that will help you become a leader of technology transformation that delivers great results for the business with ease.

This framework aligns with Intel IT's strategic planning approach, outlined in its whitepaper, *Aligning IT with Business Goals through Strategic Planning*.[3] In order to

---

3    Intel Corporation, "Aligning IT with Business Goals through Strategic Planning", *Whitepaper Intel Information Technology, December 2008*

align the IT business better with its overarching strategic goals and objectives, Intel made three core changes to its planning approach:

- Integrating the strategic planning calendar with the Intel corporate planning cycle, keeping Intel IT activities aligned and synchronised with the company's direction.

- Consolidating expertise and ideas from across Intel IT, bringing together a variety of perspectives in an efficient manner.

- Responding to changes in the industry by evaluating and adjusting the plan on a regular basis, helping to ensure the strategic plan is always up to date.

All three of these steps are very much aligned with the four-step framework I am about to share with you. This framework is designed to help you gain better control over the changes happening within your business as well as those taking place in the wider marketplace. These steps can help you set up the foundation for your technology innovation journey.

The four steps are:

# STEP 1: CLARITY

Engaging the broader organisation as early as possible in order to gather the business requirements for your technology innovation is a great way to ensure you choose the best possible solution for the business in the short and in the long term.

Also a good technology solution will have created significant business benefits for other organisations in the past. By building relationships with and gaining as much insight as possible from the organisations that went before you, you can leverage what did work, avoid what didn't and realise even more business benefits during and post implementation.

# STEP 2: CONTEXT

A good leader of change has a clear vision of what he or she wants to achieve with the implementation of a new technology solution. This step is about assessing the strategic business goals against the new technology capability and helps to create a simple but compelling vision. This vision explains why you choose to invest in a certain technology solution and how it will lead to improvements across the business. Having this context will help you communicate to the broader organisation, will reduce or even prevent potential resistance and will lower the likelihood of doubling up on work to achieve the same goals.

# STEP 3: COLLABORATION

Key to the successful implementation of any change is transparency and collaboration, both within the project team and across the business as a whole. By communicating openly about your vision and what you want to achieve with the new technology solution, you will secure buy-in as well as be able to gather further insights on how this change can benefit the organisation and what obstacles to look out for.

This step is also apparent in Intel's three changes, the second being 'consolidating experience and expertise' from across the organisation.

Considering the propensity for silos in large financial services companies, collaboration ensures that rather than technology solutions being built to resolve one business issue, solutions can meet business-wide needs and become more successfully embedded across the organisation.

# STEP 4: CONTROL

As a leader it is important to feel confident and in control of what is happening within your business and what external factors may impact your business. It is important to consider changes in the broader organisation as well as outside the organisation that could have a potential impact on your technology innovation journey. Having a robust risk management approach gives you structure and insight into what risks are being identified and how they relate to other movements inside as well as outside the business. This gives you the confidence you need to proactively guide the project as well as manage any other changes that are happening in and around the business.

Again this aligns with Intel's approach, with the third change to their strategic planning being staying on top of the ever-changing marketplace and the rapid evolution of technology in general.

# THE BENEFITS

This four-step framework provides you with practical steps you can take to successfully lead change in your business. Some of the benefits are:

- You will be able to make more informed decisions quicker and not just in relation to your technology innovation project, but also in relation to your broader business.

- You will be able identify risks earlier and manage them more proactively.

- You will be able to learn from other organisations that have already implemented the same technology and prevent making the same mistakes as well as implement those practices that really worked.

- You will be able to discover more about the technology solution up front and therefore uncover more about the functionality that you may want to use in your business.

- You will be able to identify the right people to support your technology transformation and help you to complete the implementation with little or no business disruption, within budget and on time.

- You will gain clarity up front on how the technology can support the business vision and strategy. This will allow you to create a compelling pitch to enlist your peers, the CEO and the board as advocates for the change. You will then be able to create alliances with other leaders across the organisation to help drive the change across the business as early as possible.

- You will have a clear stakeholder engagement plan in place to guide where and when you need to communicate and interact with staff in order to make sure the broader organisation continues to work in alignment with your vision.

- You will have the right processes in place to ensure risk is managed on an ongoing basis and you are kept up to date on all aspects in relation to the progress of the technology implementation. You will be able to reflect on changes happening in the broader organisation that could potentially have an impact on the project.

- Last but not least, you will gain deeper insight into your leadership style and where you can make improvements in order to make a bigger and more positive impact on your employees and the organisation.

# WHO AM I?

For the past fifteen years I have worked on multi-million dollar enterprise-wide change programs for large blue chip organisations, including Sterigenics, Valvoline, Qantas, NAB, Westpac and AMP. I have worked on technology innovation programs such as replacing an enterprise-wide resource planning system, implementing a master data management system, creating a new online asset management tool and other technology innovations.

Over this time I have experienced firsthand what a difference it makes if change is led effectively. I have seen the relief on people's faces when they are given answers to their questions so they can better understand the change before it happens. I've seen how this reduces resistance and eliminates the assumptions and misconceptions people create if they don't have enough information.

I have also experienced what happens when there is a lack of clarity around *why* a change is happening and why such a significant amount of money is being spent in one part of the business and not elsewhere. I have seen what happens when there is no clear direction from the senior leadership of an organisation. I have also seen the struggle and chaos that can ensue when leaders have no vision or strategy for the change, which is incredibly unsettling and stressful for everyone involved.

I remember when I first experienced real change. It was when my parents decided I needed new furniture for my room. I must have been about eleven or twelve and

I needed a bigger desk before going to high school. Because it was very hard to find a matching desk for my bedroom furniture, my parents decided that we needed to replace everything. Not only did they decide to replace the furniture, they also thought it was time for some new wallpaper and paint as well. We quickly found a desk with bed and a closet to match, and before long my safe haven had been completely restyled and had a very different look and feel. While I was involved in selecting the furniture and the wallpaper, I still struggled with adjusting to the new environment.

I believe I was quite upset at first, as to this day I can recall how I felt quite lost without my old surroundings. I no longer felt comfortable in the one place in the house that was mine.

Even though I've experienced significant change since then, including studying and working around the world, I don't think I deal with change very well. I have found that when a change takes me by surprise, I really don't feel right. I feel lost and unsettled.

In a more recent experience, we had to change floors at work. We were moving to a floor that was newly refurbished with the most up-to-date technology available to promote collaboration and efficient team work. Based on what I knew about myself, I expected to struggle with this transition, but I found myself comfortably adjusting from day one.

I believe it had everything to do with the level of communication about this transition, which started months prior, as well as the introduction to other floors that looked similar to the floor we would move to. There were also very few people that resisted the change, and those who did resist were largely the people who had not read the relevant communications in preparation for the move or didn't attend the introductions to other similar floors.

There was also a very clear link with the overall business strategy of becoming a more agile organisation, increasing collaboration and improving the way we help the customer. Leaders from around the organisation kept referring to this vision throughout the year and linking it to our changing workspaces. Leaders were visible in regular town hall meetings and were well informed about the changes to the workplace and the progress of moving the different teams to those newly refurbished floors. Leaders also shared the challenges of the move to the new floors and the ongoing improvements and learnings they were gathering from the teams that were already working on the new floors. It was clear that leaders were listening and were creating an open, transparent and honest dialogue with all employees to ensure the changes were effective and being embraced by all.

When leaders create clarity around the vision behind a change and share it frequently with their teams and the broader organisation, people feel more at ease about the inevitable uncertainties of change. In some cases, leaders have the ability to create such an open, transparent and honest dialogue that people will barely notice the challenges and will simply be excited about what is coming. It inspires me to see great leaders have such an effect on people. It creates a sense of security in times of change, as they can rely on the leader telling them exactly what is happening and why. While these leaders may not have all the answers up front, they share what they do know openly and welcome feedback.

The end result? Staff can more easily adapt to an ever-changing environment. Leaders can remove the anxiety surrounding change, create peace of mind and encourage increased collaboration to build sustainable change through inspiring leadership.

When people are more at ease, their productivity will not diminish during times of change. Instead, productivity will go up as people want to contribute to the vision and want to be part of the organisation's future. This not only reduces the cost of potential business disruption due to change, it also increases the likelihood of change projects running on time and within budget.

## IT'S TIME TO BECOME A LEADER OF CHANGE

I would like to challenge you as a successful leader in the industry to rethink your role in leading technology change. I would like to motivate you to reflect on your leadership style and learn how to become even more effective at leading your people and leading transformation in your organisation.

Reading books, taking courses and asking for feedback takes courage and initiative but, if you do, this is a very encouraging sign to your subordinates. It shows that you are willing to learn as a leader; that you are willing to improve and develop as much as you ask your people to push themselves and improve their performance.

Above and beyond this book's four-step framework, your leadership can make the biggest difference of all, keeping the project team focused and keeping the organisation involved and thinking proactively about the changes that the new technology will bring and the risks involved. This will potentially make the difference between a technology solution that may be another disappointment and a technology solution that exceeds your organisation's objectives.

The financial services industry is in a state of flux, and it is paramount that senior leaders take an active role in managing these changes by being visible, communicating the vision behind the change and maintaining oversight of the change throughout the implementation. If you do, you will not only achieve great results for your organisation, but you will inspire and empower your people to make great things happen.

This book is the first step.

# Step 1: **Clarity**

*'The important thing is to not stop questioning. Curiosity has its own reason for existing.'*

*— Albert Einstein*

To kick off this first step, I would like to provide you with some examples where technology implementations did not achieve the desired business results.

Avon Products Inc. is an American manufacturer and direct selling company of beauty, household and personal care products. Avon was founded in 1886 and in 2013 its revenue was recorded as US$9.95 billion. In 2009, Avon decided to invest in a highly sophisticated enterprise-wide resource planning software, which they first rolled out in Canada to later be extended globally.

However, the front end of the software was not user-friendly enough, which made it difficult for staff to adopt and embrace the new technology. As a result, the software implementation started disrupting regular operations and caused Avon staff to leave the company in 'meaningful numbers'.

Following this, the company decided to put further implementation of the software on hold. Avon was forced to write down between US$100 million and US$125 million on its balance sheet due the system not being rolled out globally, as was intended.[4]

A similar example is Nike's attempt to implement a new supply chain management system. Nike was investing in a demand planning system that would empower the company to predict sales. However, this didn't align with

---

4    Ben Kepes, "Avon's Failed SAP Implementation A Perfect Example Of The Enterprise IT Revolution", Forbes 17 December 2013

Nike's business model, which relies on tightly controlling their athletic footwear supply chain and committing retailers to orders far in advance.

By contrast, demand planning is a combination of systems and gauging retailer interest to determine the type and quantity of footwear to be supplied. Nike decided to turn off the demand planning component of the software for all but one of its product lines (apparel).

The failed technology implementation cost Nike more than US$100 million in lost sales, depressed its stock price by twenty per cent, triggered a number of class-action lawsuits and caused its Chairman, President and CEO, Phil Knight, to famously state, 'This is what you get for $400 million, huh? A speed bump'.[5]

Both Avon and Nike's implementation failures could have been avoided with more research up front and better management of the changes in the business.

In Avon's case, if the user-friendliness of the application was thoroughly researched and tested prior to signing up to the multi-year, multi-million dollar investment, and if staff were engaged, trained and educated from the beginning of the project (more on this in Step 3), the project could have been managed to a degree that would have at least resulted in fewer good staff resigning, less business disruption and the prevention of significant write offs. I would even go on to say that I believe it could have resulted in a successful

---

5    Christopher Koch, "Nike Rebounds: How (and Why) Nike Recovered from Its Supply Chain Disaster", CIO 15 June 2004

implementation and the global roll-out would have been pursued based on the business benefits realised with the pilot in Canada.

In Nike's case, there seems to have been insufficient understanding of the technology up front and there was insufficient consideration as to how that functionality would support the existing business model. Senior management was probably intelligently aware of the need to improve efficiencies in their supply chain processes. However due to not really understanding the capability enough, didn't consider some aspects of the technology would simply contradict crucial aspects of the way they do business with their retailers.

There is often a missed opportunity to understand more about the technology that is being considered up front. Understanding more about the technology can help with ensuring it actually is suitable for your business, will resolve the business issues that are driving the need for the new technology and, most importantly, will help enable the business strategy by fulfilling your customers' needs.

When an organisation chooses to invest in a new technology solution, there will be one or more organisations that have gone before them and they will have learnings that can be used to minimise the risk of failing again.

Most technology vendors are asked to provide 'reference sites' that are willing to share their learnings and experiences about the technology solution, as well as insights regarding the implementation of the technology in their organisation. These reference sites are generally not immediate competitors and conversations focus on the quality of the technology solution and the service provided by the vendor.

In my experience, this step often doesn't get the attention it deserves. Generally the focus of conversations with reference sites is the service provided by the vendor, the scope of the functionality that was implemented and the ease with which the technology was implemented for the client.

While these are important questions to ask, are they digging deeply enough?

One of the most common mistakes I see in leading technology driven change is that senior leaders often don't know enough about the technology solution they are investing in. A business case for releasing funding in order to invest in the technology is mainly focused on resolving existing business issues and often does not explore the potential for the organisation to benefit further from the technology.

If you were buying yourself a new phone, wouldn't you want to know exactly how the new phone stacked up against your old one, what features and functionality it had and how it was a step up from your former model? Of course – while the trigger for replacing your old phone might have been that it kept 'dying on you', if you're investing in a new one anyway you would want it to give you new and improved functionality. You would want to be able to do more with your phone than before and for it to create efficiency and convenience in your life that you didn't have before.

It is no different to when you invest in new technology solutions. Being able to invest a large sum of money in new technology should be seen as a great opportunity to make a real difference in your business.

On that note do you think that gathering as much information as possible from these reference sites on how the technology has contributed to their business, how the implementation was conducted and what worked and didn't work would be valuable? I appreciate that not all organisations are willing to share this type of information. However, I believe it would be worth exploring and investing in building a relationship with these reference sites, as all learnings can set your business up for a greater chance of successfully embedding the new technology.

When it comes to your technology change, ask yourself:

- Do you believe that engaging the broader organisation early on and learning from your employees about their technology and business process challenges can help you make better technology innovation decisions along the way?

- Do you believe that learning more about the technology solution up front, how it works in other organisations and how it could add value to your business could give you a better chance at successfully embedding the new technology?

- Do you believe that partnering with other organisations and learning about their technology innovation projects can improve your chances of realising the business benefits you are seeking to achieve?

By doing this research and gaining a better understanding of the technology and what it has achieved for other organisations, you can create a more realistic view of the business benefits that can be achieved and provide a more prudent starting point when it comes to the challenges and risks that can be expected.

Having this clarity up front will then assist in engaging key stakeholders from around the organisation to support the technology transformation.

Step 1 involves engaging the broader organisation up front to gather information about technology related issues and opportunities, understanding the existing technology landscape, establishing a relationship with reference sites, gathering valuable insights about the technology capability and compiling all of those learnings.

## GATHERING THE BUSINESS REQUIREMENTS

Having a clear view of your business's requirements for any new technology is paramount. Think about buying a laptop. Investing in a new laptop requires you to think about the functional improvements you would like the new laptop to have in comparison to your former laptop. To assess this, you would need to be crystal clear about how you are going to use the new laptop, who is going to use the laptop, what applications you will install and use on it, how important speed is to you and the compatibility with other technology you may want to integrate with the laptop.

All of these aspects can be categorised under your (business) requirements for the technology solution. Now I am not suggesting that having a clear view of your business requirements and the benefits you want to realise can prevent anything from not going to plan during the project implementation. This is not a silver bullet. What I am saying is that, in my experience, a lack of clarity around why the business invests in a large-scale technology transformation often results in business disappointment and therefore being very clear about your business requirements up front, is very important.

The two areas to consider when gathering your business requirements are technology related issues within the business, as well as technology related opportunities for growing and improving your business.

The mistake that many organisations make is investing in technology to (just) solve business issues and pain points rather than for the purpose of innovation. However, even though these inefficiencies are very important considerations, it's just as important to consider how the solution will help the business grow and improve.

Very often the long-term benefits of a new technology solution or even the hidden cost of leaving certain functionality untouched are not sufficiently explored at the start of the implementation. Instead, decisions are made throughout the implementation based on short-term costs and short-term benefits, which can have a detrimental impact by eliminating the potential to experience further benefits down the track.

As in any organisation, there are always plenty of issues and opportunities that are screaming for attention. The most obvious issues are the ones that are directly related to customer complaints or to the sales figures.

Some of these issues and opportunities could be:

- Customer service processing times are too long.
- Customer requests are processed incorrectly (human and/ or system error).
- Customers who have expressed interest in products or services are not captured correctly and opportunity to assist them is lost.
- Finance reporting takes too long and is often not accurate.
- Customer's online experience is suboptimal.

However, it is important to dig a little deeper and consult the broader organisation on what technology issues they are experiencing in their part of the business. This broader picture of the organisation's challenges can provide a more meaningful foundation for identifying the best technology solution.

Some of the things that you could uncover are:

- Systems overwriting good data with bad data, which causes rework and can impact customer experience.

- Products or services not being sold due to negative experiences signing up to these products or services (potentially caused by the administration systems and related processes).

- Certain product systems can't store the most basic customer details (such as an email address), which means important customer information is lost.

- Some system functionality is bypassed as it is not fit for purpose, which means clunky and time consuming business processes exist to get a job done.

- A business division is investing in a new reporting capability to improve not only the look and feel of reports, but also increase the accuracy and richness of data represented in the report. This same capability could potentially be leveraged by other parts of the business, if they knew it was available.

A practical example can be the improvements made to or even the replacement of a Customer Relationship Management (CRM) system.

This generally is a crucial part of the business, which often highlights inefficiencies in how customers are being served and provides a source of customer complaints.

However, when deciding to invest in either improving your existing CRM system or replacing it for a better and more innovative solution, the focus should not just be on the inefficiencies of the existing system, but the opportunities that innovating the existing system or even buying a new system will bring.

Questions that you could ask yourself and your team are:

- Is there an opportunity to remove unnecessary steps in our customer service process through innovating the system?

- Would there be an opportunity to capture new and richer data from our customers, which we currently can't, but our customers are willing to provide?

- Can we be more concise about how we capture our data from interactions with our customers so it can more easily be used for analytics and better decision-making?

- Can we reduce the risk of human error by innovating the system?

- Is there an opportunity to create integrations with other valuable systems within the organisation, which currently do not exist?

- How do all of the reasons for innovation of our system(s) align with and enable our short- and long-term business strategy?

In 2004, Qantas launched Project Jetsmart, an A$40million parts management system that was seen as an important investment in new information technology systems to drive the company's maintenance, repair and overhaul operations.

However, from the start of the project Qantas struggled with a lack of buy-in from staff and the unions. The unions claimed that the software was increasing the employees' workload and went as far as to give the mechanics at Qantas the advice to 'not assist with the implementation'.[6]

The unions make it very difficult for Qantas to engage with their employees directly. If the unions understood the reasons why the organisation wanted to innovate and were consulted prior to the commitment to the technology innovation project, do you think they would have been more collaborative?

If Qantas had engaged the unions early on in their preliminary thinking, they may have even assisted with gathering business requirements for the technology innovation. They would have been able to give valuable

---

6   Michael Krigsman, "Qantas Airways, a perfect storm for IT failure?", *Beyond IT failure*, ZDNet, 29 February 2008

insight into what the workforce would require in order to improve the efficiency and effectiveness of businesses processes.

Finally, if the unions were engaged before crucial decisions were made, they could have been advocates for the change and helped the organisation on-board employees on the journey and adopt the new technology solution.

Instead, the unions created a hostile environment where Qantas employees became the enemies of management.

Input from the broader organisation can be of great benefit to not only choosing the right solution for the organisation, but also in the creation of change advocacy.

As a result, the business requirements gathered for the technology investment must reflect, or at least have considered, all relevant views within the organisation (particularly if the technology is going to be implemented enterprise-wide).

In order to gain insight into organisation-wide technology issues and opportunities, it is worth opening up the communication to a bigger audience for example via a questionnaire.

You can start gathering information from stakeholders across the organisation from the moment you start gathering business requirements for the technology innovation. Starting the communication with the broader organisation early on has many advantages, some of which include:

- When engaged at an early stage of the project, people feel valued for their opinion and feel included in whatever changes the organisation needs to make.

- You will gain a wealth of knowledge and very diverse views and opinions about the technology challenges across the organisation, which will better inform the decisions you need to make.

- You can reduce the risk of duplicating effort by not working in a siloed manner. Often different parts of the business face similar challenges and launch initiatives with similar goals due to a lack of transparent communication between business units. Ultimately, these initiatives may create conflicting outcomes.

When it comes to more detailed input and feedback, some of the people in the organisation you would want to communicate with include:

- Your peers.

- Your direct reports.

- Leaders and managers of the areas of the business that will likely be impacted by the change.

- The CEO and CIO.

- Leaders and managers in the IT department, specifically those who support the current technology solution, which you might be intending to upgrade or replace.

- Solution architects.

As a general rule, the people who work with the technology every day will bring the most valuable information to the surface. For example customer service staff and administrative staff will be able to provide insight into the frustrations that customers face each time they interact with the business due to systems not operating effectively. Product managers can provide great insight into the challenges they face monitoring what products or services are doing well and what products and services are not.

### Muneesh Wadhwa, Founder of
### Humanity in Business, says:

*"Inspiring leaders focus on helping their stakeholders get better outcomes, thereby ensuring sustainable business growth. These leaders always put employees, internal and external customers, suppliers and the wider community at the core of their decisions to ensure high levels of engagement and as a result, excellent long term performance."*

It takes guts to open up communication this early on in your technology innovation journey, but what do you have to lose? Based on the wealth of knowledge you gather from people in different parts of the organisation, the leadership team can determine which of the business challenges will achieve the biggest return on investment and have the greatest positive impact on the business overall.

# THE EXISTING TECHNOLOGY LANDSCAPE

Besides gathering business requirements before going out into the market and looking at technology solutions, it is also important to understand the existing technology landscape in the organisation.

Often there are huge challenges with technology innovation due to heritage systems and Band-Aid approaches to fixing or improving functionality, and another Band-Aid solution may be more likely to hinder than help. Instead, consider how the existing technology landscape may be contributing to the problems you discover, and whether a more holistic solution may be required.

Technology experts in your business can assist with this detailed analysis and can play an important role in analysing the different technology solutions that you are considering investing in. However, be mindful to not rely solely on the technology view of the world – make sure to overlay this knowledge with the business outcomes you want to achieve.

This is a mistake that I have seen on many occasions, where a technology solution might be the best fit from an infrastructure perspective or even from a technology vendor perspective (considering most organisations have preferred technology partners), but this doesn't always mean the best return on investment from a business outcome perspective.

# BUILD A RELATIONSHIP WITH REFERENCE SITES

Once you have gathered your business requirements, you can look in the market for a suitable technology solution. The technology vendors will provide you with details of organisations (reference sites) that have implemented the solution successfully in the past.

There are significant benefits to be gained from investing time and energy in establishing an ongoing relationship with these reference sites in order to be able to leverage their knowledge of the technology solution as well as the implementation of the solution into the future. A reference site can offer valuable insights during the implementation process about how to overcome obstacles, challenges with customisation of the solution and for example understanding how best to collaborate with the vendor. Ideally, senior leadership should connect with the senior leaders of the reference site and establish a potential collaboration up front before interviewing them on the vendor and technology capabilities.

Any relationship needs to have benefits for both parties, therefore, consider what you can offer in return to this organisation. Before starting the conversation about the technology solution and vendor, it is worth exploring up front if there could be a potential exchange of valuable information.

If an exchange of value can be agreed upon, and clear expectations are set, a great collaboration can be established. There may be a possibility for a long-term partnership where the reference site can assist you with your technology implementation and, in return, you can provide them with other valuable information or advice.

A few things are very important in order to prevent either business to feel let down by the partnership in any way. You need to ensure that your expectations are very clear from both sides, your values are aligned, there is no conflict of interest, there is no competitive risk, there is trust and most importantly there is something to gain from the engagement for both businesses.

Once you have a view of how both parties can contribute to the engagement in the longer term, it is worth checking with your legal team to assess if any agreements need to be documented in contractual form in order to protect your business as well as the reference site.

# RESEARCH KEY AREAS

Even though every organisation is very different and the way the technology will integrate within the existing systems and business processes will vary, at a high level there are always similarities. These similarities include reasons why implementations fail, common learnings, the technology solution's capability and the solution's potential.

When it comes to failures or challenges, one approach is being aware of the common challenges in technology implementations, or the reasons why they fail, and then interviewing your reference sites about how they tackled these areas.

According to the 2013 white paper *Top 5 Reasons ERP Implementations Fail and What You Can Do about It* by Ziff Davis B2B,[7] common reasons for failure include:

- Setting unrealistic expectations from the outset.
- Failure to manage organisational change.
- Not involving key stakeholders.
- Poor project management.
- Failure to manage business benefits.

Similarly, there are often common learnings that can be found for each type of technology implementation, regardless of the organisation performing the implementation. Some examples could be:

- Key considerations and findings from an architecture review.
- The structure of the technology vendor agreement (e.g. agreement based on

7    Ziff Davis B2B, "Top 5 Reasons ERP Implementations Fail and What You Can Do About It", Whitepaper 2013

set price, including ongoing support at a variable rate).

- The effectiveness of the business implementation plan and execution.

The next area to consider is the capability of the new technology solution and how it can help your organisation not only improve on existing issues and challenges, but also help change the way the business operates, realise benefits in the long term as well as creating more added value for the customer.

These benefits may include:

- Reducing cost.
- Increasing business efficiency.
- Addressing ageing technology.
- Improving customer experience.
- Creation of new business opportunities (for example, improved online services for customers).

Finally, the *potential* of the new technology is often not thoroughly researched up front. The focus, in my experience, is about resolving known business issues and inefficiencies as well as market-driven technology innovation requirements. Not often does a business look more broadly at the technology capability and identify other (less obvious) potential benefits of the new technology.

The end result is that potential benefits are not uncovered until the implementation itself, at which point it may be too late to take advantage of them.

Not everything can be known up front, as each organisation has a different technology landscape as well as different information flowing through their systems. However, the more you know about the technology in advance, the better prepared you will be to make crucial decisions about functionality down the track. Keep in mind that your research of these areas doesn't need to be limited to the reference sites. You can also research these questions online using technology reviews, blogs and articles, which can provide interesting insights about vendors as well as the technology capability.

## COMPILE YOUR LEARNINGS

Once you have gathered this mountain of information, it is important to create a short, simplified summary of key findings and learnings so you can share the information easily and effectively across your organisation. This summary will be a great leveraging tool to demonstrate your thorough research as well as to educate your peers and team on the technology solution and how it can help the organisation achieve its objectives.

To ensure your summary has the right level of information and answers the questions of key stakeholders when deciding on a new technology solution, you should start with linking the gathered information to your business requirements (the identified business issues and opportunities).

You could even decide to prioritise the business requirements based on the return on investment, level of importance to enable the business strategy and also the feasibility to resolve it with the new technology capability.

Once you have this as a starting point, it will be easier to link the relevant information about your existing technology landscape, the technology capability you are looking to implement and the learnings from the reference sites.

The output of this step would be a summary of approximately four to six pages describing case studies provided by the reference sites, the business benefits achieved with the new technology, the core technology functionality and capability, and key learnings from the reference sites regarding the technology implementation.

The case study (or studies) should include:

- **The background of the organisation**: When they were founded, their core product or service and the size of the business when they decided to implement the technology solution.

- **Similarities between the reference site and your organisation:** This will demonstrate the relevance of the learnings you have gathered. These similarities may include typical organisational qualities such as the type of industry, type of customer and size of the organisation, or they may include less obvious aspects such as what business outcomes the reference site was trying to achieve or what business challenges they were trying to resolve with the technology.

The discussion on business benefits should be compared to what the organisation initially set out to achieve with the technology implementation. The business benefits should include one or more of the following aspects:

- **Operational efficiency:** Attracting or maintaining skilled and motivated staff, optimisation of business processes, staff productivity, managing business change programs effectively and so on.

- **Return on investment:** Creating more financial transparency, optimisation of business process costs, optimisation of products and services costs, continued investment from shareholders and more.

- **Competitive advantage**: The organisation's agility to respond to market trends and implement changes, increasing the demand for products and services, increasing the organisation's customer focus and business innovation.

- **Risk reduction**: Compliance with internal policies and external laws and regulations, business resiliency, strategic risk-based decision making and so on.

The technology solution capability should:

- Stipulate the functionality that comes 'out of the box' (this is the technology implemented without any customisation).

- Describe what customised functionality the organisation has added and for what business purpose.

Lastly, and this stage is often missed, it's important to share insights on how the organisation implemented the technology and other key learnings which can assist you with your implementation.

This can include:

- How much time they took for the implementation.

- Their approach (agile, waterfall, a phased approach and so on).

- Any business risks that were identified along the way.

- What new functionality they uncovered during the implementation.

- The collaboration with the vendor.

- Unexpected cost that was incurred.

- Challenges with integrating into an existing technology landscape.

- Transitioning to business-as-usual once the functionality was successfully implemented.

As I mentioned earlier, it is worth exploring if a more long-term engagement can be established with the reference site in order to consult them throughout the implementation.

There are so many surprises that simply cannot be pre-empted at the start of the project, which would be beneficial to be able to discuss with an organisation that has done it before.

Finally, when you collate this information it is important to be conscious of the language used and the information is presented in a very concise manner. With technology innovation it is easy to get bogged down by jargon and complex technology speak. This results into the communication of ambiguous information, which can cause misalignment between key stakeholders right from the start.

Even worse the lack of clear and concise messaging about the technology solution can cause people to make up their own mind about what the technology can do and create incorrect expectations. It is very hard to correct these expectations and re-educate people later on.

## *KEY TAKEAWAYS*

1. Engage the broader organisation to identify issues and opportunities to form the foundation of business requirements for your technology innovation.

2.  Learn as much as possible about the technology up front by leveraging the knowledge and experience of reference sites provided by the technology vendor.

3.  When compiling your learnings, focus on linking the gathered information to your organisation's issues, requirements and opportunities to ensure key stakeholders see the benefits of the technology change.

# Step 2: **Context**

*'If you cannot explain it simply, you don't understand it well enough.'*

*– Albert Einstein*

.

After completing Step 1, you now have a set of business requirements, some knowledge about the technology capability you're considering, an understanding of the best practices from reference sites on how to implement the technology, as well as an understanding of what business benefits can be achieved. You can now create a clear vision for the technology transformation to share with the broader business.

In this step you will overlay the insights you gained in Step 1 with the context of the business strategy and vision for the short and for the long term. This includes defining and prioritising your key business drivers, sharing your key business drivers with the broader organisation, creating a vision for your technology innovation journey and creating a roadmap for the change.

Having this level of clear vision for the technology transformation as early as possible will put you on the front foot for managing the technology transformation in your business and set you up as a leader of change.

## DEFINING AND PRIORITISING THE KEY BUSINESS DRIVERS FOR THE CHANGE

In order to start working towards a clear vision for your technology transformation, it is important to be very clear about the key business drivers for this investment. These business drivers are specific to your organisation or even business division and they need to be assessed against the broader organisation's objectives, competitive pressures, market trends, technology innovation in other parts of the business and the overarching business vision and strategy.

In Step 1 we discussed gathering your business *requirements* and even though that is critical input into this step to defining your key business *drivers*, please do not confuse the two. The business requirements you gathered in Step 1 will be at a detailed level the functionality you need to improve in your business. The key business drivers will represent the benefits of that functionality at a more strategic level.

 For example in Step 1 you would have determined that the business needs to be able to capture customer details consistently across all product systems. This requirement can support the overarching business driver to 'make your customers feel like you know them' by being able to gather more rich contact information across all the different products and services they might have with your business.

It is very important to agree on the key business drivers as well as prioritise them based on importance to the business, before or as early as possible in your technology innovation journey.

This provides further context for your technology innovation and can be exceptionally useful when technology design decisions have to be made. Also when the feasibility of the implementation is at risk and certain parts of the capability can't be delivered or trade-offs have to be made, these key business drivers can provide the guidance to stay true to the original intent of the technology innovation.

Staying in line with the example I provided in Step 1, an example of a trade-off could be when you are implementing a new Customer Relationship Management (CRM) system in order to increase the efficiency of the customer service department and reduce cost. While implementing the new system, it becomes clear that the integration of the new CRM system won't work well with the central data warehouse. Changes to the infrastructure have to be made in order to ensure that all the data from the new CRM system will flow through to the data warehouse in order to be able to report on this data and use it in valuable customer insights and other types of management reporting. If the (only) key driver for this project was to improve the efficiency of the customer service department, the additional cost to improve the infrastructure and make sure that data was flowing through to the data warehouse, would not be approved.

However if your business wants to improve its customer service and get to know their customer better, this additional information that is gathered with the new CRM system is crucial to the future of the business and well worth the additional investment as well as the potential delay of the project.

### *Paul Franks, Director, Financial Services at SAS Australia & New Zealand says:*

*"Success can't be timed, quality has to be there, sustainability has to be there and particularly how does every decision support and enable business transition post project."*

Some other examples of key business drivers could be:

- Reduce IT cost (for example reducing system maintenance cost by further system integration and optimisation).

- Improve data driven decision-making (by increasing reporting capability and accuracy).

- Improve customer experience.

Once you have defined a list of key business drivers both to resolve issues within the business as well as pursue opportunities to improve and grow the business, it is important to be clear on their priorities.

When a decision needs to be made and there are two key business drivers impacted, it needs to be clear which one has the highest priority.

Consider my previously mentioned example where the project was trying to increase efficiency in the customer service department and reduce cost. When the opportunity arose to invest more in the solution in order to gain better customer insights and reporting, it has to be clear if cost reduction supersedes the need for better reporting.

The prioritisation of your key business drivers will be driven by your overarching business strategy and vision and it is valuable to agree the prioritisation of these drivers up front.

Defining your key business drivers up front based on business challenges as well as business opportunities, prioritising these business drivers based on value add to the business and aligning it with your short and long-term business strategy, will provide you the critical foundation for any decision-making along your technology innovation journey.

The clearer you are on your key business drivers and the more transparent you are communicating them within your business, the less likely bad decisions will be made during the course of your technology implementation.

## THE VALUE OF SHARING YOUR KEY BUSINESS DRIVERS FOR THE CHANGE

I once worked on a project that was implementing a new master data management system. The key drivers for this technology innovation, which was later referred to as 'open heart surgery', was the fact that the quality, accuracy and completeness of customer information was very poor. Less than thirty-five per cent of its customers' mobile phone numbers were correctly captured in the company's systems while incorrect address details caused customers (and non-customers) to complain about incorrect mail delivery.

Not only was it paramount for this organisation to know its customers and be able to contact them, it was also costing the organisation money due to the sheer amount of return mail, as well as the fixes and rework that needed to take place on an ongoing basis in order to correct customer information.

As we were halfway into implementing the solution for the first foundational release, the business uncovered new capabilities the technology solution could offer that had not been in the original project scope. These were aspects such as the centralisation and automation of data governance requirements, as well as functionality to overcome historical customer data issues such as the combining of a husband and wife as one customer.

As more business stakeholders learned about the new technology, more and more questions arose regarding what the new technology solution was delivering for the business and what it wasn't. A major concern was whether this new technology was going to resolve any of their business efficiency issues or customer services challenges and if it was really going to achieve the business benefits it had set out to achieve.

In order to answer this growing number of questions about what the solution really was going to do for the business, we created a one-page summary and described what the technology was going to provide in business terms. Even though it was a valuable exercise to pull together the one-page document about what the master data management system would and wouldn't deliver, it was too late to change the design of the solution. Considering the implementation of the master data management solution was an investment of A\$21 million over eighteen months, up front engagement with key stakeholders could have resulted in a more complete list of requirements and a better use of these funds based on the business's strategy.

On another project, an organisation was introducing a brand new analytical capability that would mean they would leapfrog the competition when it came to its ability to produce insights into their customers. The technology would make these insights available to business users across the enterprise in an easy-to-use and interactive way.

However, months after the capability was launched, it became clear that several other parts of the business were trying to achieve the same thing for their business divisions. The challenge the business owner of the analytics service faced was that he had to quickly communicate the message that this service was an enterprise-wide service.

A high-level stakeholder pack was developed to start communicating to the wider organisation that this capability had been launched and was still being developed, yet no clarity could be provided as to when these business stakeholders could become customers of this service and come knocking on the door to request specific insights.

While connecting with stakeholders (a more detailed approach is described in Step 3) up front won't prevent all potential resistance, it will help reduce them while preventing a siloed approach to change and creating enthusiasm throughout the business. I've found that, as people learn more about the new technology, they become excited about its potential and, equally important, they want to help.

As stakeholders get excited, they start to ask more questions. These questions help them get more of an understanding about what the new technology can do, and what it can do for them. This gives you a valuable opportunity to gain further insight into challenges around the business that the new technology solution might be able to address. If you can't address some of the things that people are bringing to your attention, you have the clarity and information at hand to provide them with the context, the reason why you are investing in this specific technology solution.

## CREATE A VISION FOR YOUR TECHNOLOGY INNOVATION JOURNEY

As I discussed in the introduction of this book, there is a significant difference between change management and change leadership. Change management is a more tactical approach to change while change leadership is a more strategic approach to change. While tactical change management is needed to help embed change on a smaller scale and for managing the risks directly related to the implementation, when it comes to big investments in large technology solutions that run across business divisions, it is important to be more strategic.

One of the key differences between change management and change leadership is whether or not there is a broader vision for the change and a roadmap to achieve that vision.

Unfortunately, in most cases organisations rely on change management rather than change leadership and there is no clear vision to guide them. The consequence is that when difficult decisions have to be made during the course of the implementation, they often make them based on technology feasibility, budget and the project timeline rather than a clear business vision for the technology innovation.

Once the implications of these decisions for the business are uncovered, it is often too late to change as the design of the solution has been locked in and there is no more budget available to reverse engineer the solution to a better outcome for the business.

This leaves stakeholders disappointed and wondering what could have been. They will feel at a loss that so much money has been spent and that the additional features that could have made their lives easier or made their jobs add more value weren't even considered. This is then compounded by the fact that most technology solution implementations stop as soon as the first round of budget submissions has run out. Within a few years, the technology falls behind and starts causing trouble to other new technology investments that are being introduced, as certain functionality hasn't been completely bedded down or further improved.

By contrast, having a clear vision will inform the business of what the solution will achieve, and will give a reason for why certain features or aspects weren't included.

This ensures not only those who are involved are on the same page, but that the broader organisation is aware of the changes being made and can collectively work towards the most rewarding outcome for the business.

As a result, I urge you to consider not just creating a short-term vision but also a longer-term vision and empower more people around the organisation to take part and ownership in the new technology innovation journey. People from all different parts of the business can come up with ideas on how to make it work for them, enable the business strategy, further improve efficiency and improve customer service.

So where do you start to create your vision for technology innovation. Based on all the information you have gathered in Step 1 and also the selection of key business drivers you have now defined, you can define the *what, why* and *when.*

Your vision should explain:

- ***What* capability the technology solution will bring to the organisation.** At a high level explain the functionality and benefits that the technology will provide. This should be closely aligned with the business requirements you gathered in Step 1. All stakeholders that provided input into the gathering of business requirements should be able to understand if their business requirements will be addressed with this new capability.

- *Why* **the organisation needs to invest in (this particular) technology innovation**. Earlier you defined and prioritised the key business drivers for your technology innovation. These key business drivers will be forming your why. This part of your vision is exceptionally powerful if it is describing in clear and easy to understand language why the organisation is going down this path. Having a clear and concise why that everyone involved can understand, will be paramount for the broader buy-in, participation and embedding of the changes that need to happen. As described earlier your key business drivers, your why should cover:

  o The business challenges you are trying to resolve (for instance, internal operating efficiency, customer service, external compliance, challenges in the marketplace and so on).

  o The business opportunities you want to pursue (such as improving customer experience, attracting new customers, increasing intelligence within the company to drive better decision making in the future and more).

  o The business benefits that can be achieved with the new technology (these may include reducing processing time, reducing work-around or rework, improving the customer experience, improving data accuracy and more).

o How the business benefits of the new technology align with the overarching business strategy (if the business strategy is focused on becoming more customer-centric, for example, how will this technology help the business become more customer-centric?).

- ***When*** **the business can expect to see these benefits**. Besides the vision describing *what* and *why*, you should support the vision with a roadmap for the change (refer to the next section 'Establish a roadmap for the change' for further detail). When the broader organisation will learn about these innovation plans, the first thing they will want to know is when they can expect these changes to happen.

# ESTABLISH A ROADMAP FOR THE CHANGE

When you communicate the 'what' and 'why' to people, the first question you will get in response is: 'When will this new capability be available?'

Once you have articulated your vision for the change, the final step is to create a roadmap to achieve it.

Your initial wish list of prioritised key business drivers may not be feasible based on limitations such as technical feasibility and cost. As a result, one of the important elements to consider is how the different business drivers are prioritised and how they need to play out in the form of a strategic roadmap.

This more detailed planning will not only help focus the implementation activities on the right elements of the solution and drive better decision making along the way, it will also inform people around the organisation of when they can expect to see what, which is important when managing expectations. Creating this roadmap to support your vision involves placing your key business drivers on a timeline.

Where your key business drivers sit on the timeline is related to:

- The way the technology solution will be implemented based on technical feasibility and integration into the existing technology landscape (for example, starting with a foundation and building more capability over time).

- The prioritisation of the key business drivers.

- The funding available for the technology innovation.

- Dependencies on other (technology driven) changes happening in the broader organisation.

In order to have clarity on all these aspects, you would need to have a workshop with parties who will have answers to the following questions:

- What part of the technology do we need to implement now based on our key business drivers?

- How much funding is available for the current financial year for this technology innovation?

- What is the proposed approach for the technology implementation?

- How much funding is required for the full implementation?

- Will the implementation go beyond the current financial year and, if so, what parts are anticipated to cross over into the next financial year?

- What is the contingency budget? (For technology innovation, contingency is considered great planning and it's worth overestimating your contingency by twenty-five to fifty per cent – technology implementations come with many surprises and, whether good or bad, they always cost money.)

- How does your list of prioritised key business drivers align with the proposed implementation approach? (This includes the consideration of what business benefits you want to achieve in the current financial year versus those that can be achieved in future.)

Once you have clarity on the implementation approach, the business benefits at each phase of the implementation and the contingency considerations, you can create a roadmap for the technology transformation.

While this roadmap does not have to be perfect up front, and will need to be revisited periodically to ensure it still aligns with current thinking and increased knowledge about the complexities surrounding the implementation, having this outline helps reassure stakeholders and keep momentum high when you can't achieve everything in one go.

## *KEY TAKEAWAYS*

1. It is important to define and prioritise the key business drivers for the technology innovation and review them against the overarching business strategy and vision to ensure it aligns with the business's goals in the short and long term.

2. If the changes involved in your technology innovation will be widespread, it is important

to articulate a clear vision of the change. A clear vision of *what* you want to achieve, *why* you want to achieve it and *when* the business benefits will be realised will establish you as a great leader of change.

# Step 3: **Collaborate**

*'No problem can be solved from the same level of consciousness that created it.'*

*— Albert Einstein*

One of the greatest examples of a transformational business leader is Ricardo Semler.

His radical and innovative business policies put accountability and responsibility with each staff member. Semler's employees write their own job descriptions, determine their own salaries, set their own production quotas and even hire their own managers. The environment he has created has made people voluntarily work overtime to meet set targets and has decreased the need for supervisors by seventy-five per cent due to much greater participation and collaboration.

The end result is that Semler turned a US$4 million company into a US$160 million company between 1980 and 2002.[8] With his controversial methods, Semler grew revenues by 600 per cent, profits by 500 per cent and productivity by 700 per cent, even while Brazil (where the business operated) was experiencing a recession.

Finally, for over two decades employee turnover has remained at an incredibly low one to two per cent a year.[9] Not many, if any, have followed in Semler's footsteps. It is a scary and highly gutsy move to give so much power to your

---

8   Drs. Kevin & Jackie Freiberg, "Semco insanity that works", Freibergs.com 2014

9   Chuck Blakeman, "Companies without managers do better by every metric", Inc., 22 July 2014

employees, being the polar opposite of the military model most companies are built on. It is also incredibly powerful.

In the previous two chapters you gathered a lot of information and you put it together in a way that is easy for stakeholders to understand. You now have a reasonable amount of knowledge and some clear material to present to the business regarding the vision for the technology solution and the implementation roadmap. With this clear context, it is now time to start collaborating with the broader organisation.

Maybe your first thought is that it is too early to start engaging the broader organisation on this topic. You may not have even signed the dotted line to invest! At the very least, you haven't started the implementation and you are still figuring out which parts of the technology you will invest in and which you might reserve for a later investment (if you invest at all).

At this early stage, you do not have a detailed roadmap, the design of the solution or a team that will be running the project.

However, early buy-in can be the difference between success and failure, or the difference between a technology solution that acts as a Band-Aid versus a solution that transforms the business.

Early on in my career as a change manager I was hired by Valvoline Netherlands to get the company re-accredited for an internationally recognised quality standard The manufacturing plant had lost their quality accreditation due to failing to pass an independent audit and retailers of Valvoline products were starting to complain that if the certification was not regained they would stop selling the products. The General Manager of Valvoline Europe was keen to get this accreditation back, but he was very clear that he did not want to do much work for it and didn't want it to take up too much time. As I started working on the project, I realised that the only way to get this accreditation across the line was with senior management buy-in. If we didn't have buy-in at that level, staff throughout the company would simply not commit to changing business processes and ensuring a consistently high-quality outcome. I took this message to the General Manager and his response was, 'Can't we buy this certificate somewhere?'

When I thought about his response, I decided the only solution was to focus on just getting the manufacturing plant re-accredited. So I suggested to the General Manager to cut Marketing and Sales out of scope for the re-accreditation and simply focus on Operations and Technical support to get the quality certification. That went down well, as it meant that Head Office didn't have to commit to any process changes.

Even though this was not a technology implementation, the lack of buy-in from the most senior leader in the organisation was clear. His focus was ensuring that retailers would continue to stock and sell Valvoline products. The accreditation was a means to that end.

However, to achieve the accreditation, the manufacturing plant needed to change the way it worked in order to pass the independent audit. As the auditor would be interviewing random people in the organisation, we needed to prepare all of the managers and team leaders with potential questions and where to find the answers. The risk was that if the General Manager had been in the audit, the auditor could have picked up on his lack of buy-in. It was clearly described in the quality standard that it was important to show there was commitment to continuous improvement, and if management hadn't bought in to that it would have been a very hard sell.

As you can see, senior management's buy-in is crucial to making everyone else in the organisation believe in the change. The commitment of leaders in the organisation then filters throughout the rest of the organisation. In the best-case scenario, these leaders may become champions of your change, and will do the work of persuading their divisions to buy in on your behalf.

In my work as a Senior Change Manager, I have experienced the level of gratitude that people express when they get information. They have often heard about changes, projects, investments and more via the grapevine but they have no understanding of what it means for them. When you give them information and they have a forum or at least a contact point where they can raise their questions and concerns, they feel included and empowered. You'll find that the more you inform people, the more supportive and engaged they become. Communication and collaboration has helped me greatly with ruling any impacts in or out of scope and minimising the anxiety people feel towards the change.

People have time to digest the information, reflect on what it means for them, contribute if applicable or simply move on with their day-to-day activities. This reduces business disruption, resistance and helps with managing the risk of the project substantially (more about risk management in Step 4).

Those assigned to assisting with the design of the new technology solution will form a strong advocacy for other parts of the business to adopt the change as well, due to their personal contribution. The more engaged they are, the more you'll find them going the extra mile to help implement the solution. They may even volunteer to put in extra hours to resolve business problems.

Meanwhile, sharing information early on will help with gathering other business viewpoints and information and creating early buy-in from your peers and your broader business team. It will also ensure that similar initiatives are not happening in parallel, which causes duplication of effort that results in wasted money and resources and can cause unnecessary and unforeseen complexities in the implementation of the solution.

Of course you will come across resistance and objections (as you will through the entire implementation process). It is likely that not everyone will buy in to the significant investment straight away. Many will want the organisation's money to go to other initiatives that help their part of the business. But don't you think knowing about these conflicts in priorities will empower you? Won't you be able to have much more informed and deeper conversations with your objecting peers on the topic because you have uncovered these objections early on?

In the past, holding back information was seen as a safer way to go, because sharing too much information would cause unrest or business disruption. These days it is empowering to know more and to be more transparent, as long as you are doing the right thing for the business overall.

The feedback you get will help you further shape the vision and strategy and will feed into the design of the solution. There are many experts in your organisation, all of whom hold a piece of the puzzle to shape the perfect technology solution for the business.

Sharing your vision and strategy early will give these experts the time to reflect on your vision, think about what it means for their part of the business and come back with valuable insights, questions and risks (which can be managed if raised early enough).

This will empower you to really make the most of this new technology investment. You will feel strengthened about the fact that you do not have to carry the responsibility for this transformation alone. Others have bought in to the vision and want to see it succeed as much as you do! They will then invest their own time and effort into making this technology transformation a success.

# COLLABORATING WITH THE BUSINESS

### *Clare Mann, Psychologist, Trainer and Communications Expert - Communicate31, says:*

*"I don't think we really know a lot about collaborative leadership, and haven't seen a lot of it. We talk about collaboration as everyone getting involved, but I don't think that's what it is, that's participation. I think when we put aside the notion of what the objective should be and bring together a creative group of people in the right context, you can achieve much more and things you wouldn't even consider arise as solutions to problems that would never have come up otherwise."*

Technology has become more complex and more cross-functional over the years, and there's no better example of this trend than the cash register. At some point, someone realised that it was important to be able to keep money secure and count the number of transactions made in a day. The cash register therefore became an invaluable asset in every shop or retail business. However, the original cash register only calculated the total amount of the sale and ensured that you could assess that against what was inside the cash register at the end of the day.

Today, the cash register has evolved into a complete operating system that allows warehouses, stores and accounting staff to oversee a business's revenue and expenses. In some restaurants, the cash register has evolved to become an automatic connection between the kitchen and the floor staff, where food starts being prepared while the waiter is still at the customer's table. The cash register also collects valuable insights about the customer's buying behaviours.

However, this evolution wouldn't have been possible without the collaboration between different parts of the business – different teams and leaders who agreed on the design, the processes and the roles and responsibilities that came with managing the day-to-day operation of the new cash register.

Imagine if a restaurant decided to invest in a new cash register – what would have happened if the accountant who initiated this new cash register system had not spoken to the head chef, the lead waiter or the purchasing department?

One word comes to mind: resistance. Other leaders in the business would have felt excluded and like their authority had been undermined when they were not consulted on the best solution for the business. More importantly, their ideas would have not been considered as part of the solution, which would not only be detrimental to the work environment but also a missed opportunity for the business.

In a restaurant with twenty to forty staff, resolving this might not be such a challenge. Perhaps the business owner would even replace any resisting employees while the implementation was underway.

In a large organisation, this could be disastrous.

Organisational silos can be detrimental to the success of any business. However, with the military model very much in place in most organisations, political power games still take place and information is not always shared as it should be.

Collaboration early on is essential for both buy-in as well as gathering a great diversity of innovative ideas for the solution.

Following are eight tips on how you can collaborate effectively with the business.

## 1. UNDERSTAND WHAT OTHER BUSINESS DIVISIONS WANT TO ACHIEVE

Most companies these days have business processes that run across different business divisions. In order to get the right outcome, collaboration between those business divisions is crucial.

It takes a bit of effort to reach out and spend time understanding what other business divisions do or what knowledge they have that you could leverage, but it is very valuable. Take the example of building a new analytical capability. One business division invests in the technology as it wants to learn more about the company's customers in order to create more personalised engagement with the customer. However, this same capability can also be leveraged by drilling into product performance and creating financial performance reporting for the business. By feeding the analytical capability with the right data, it can create all kinds of insights.

While the first business division is implementing the capability to create better customer insights, other business divisions are looking at how to improve their systems to create better reporting or even engaging vendors to build a new solution for them to improve their reporting.

Resources are allocated to do the research and explore the options and soon a few million dollars have been spent to make a recommendation. In the meantime another business division is well underway with developing the new analytics capability, but has simply not been sharing this strategy with other business divisions. The company ends up duplicating effort, wasting time and wasting money. If times were tough for this organisation, this could kill the business.

Already in Step 1 you will have engaged various stakeholders in the business to determine what their priorities are and whether they can be addressed by your technology innovation.

If the innovation can address these priorities, your task now is to communicate how the change will address their needs. If it will not, your task is to communicate why those priorities aren't being addressed (or aren't being addressed *now*), as well as what your solution will achieve instead.

## 2. MANAGE THE HUMAN ELEMENT OF CHANGE

Large-scale changes are challenging because they are unpredictable. With so many moving pieces, it's not uncommon for the vision or roadmap to be adjusted or for challenges to crop up. This then creates uncertainty for the organisation.

People don't deal well with uncertainty as uncertainty is very hard to manage. Uncertainty makes people unsettled and can result in attitude and behavioural issues regarding the change.

Instead, the more you can provide clarity and context around the change and implementation, the more that uncertainty will reduce. The more you can plan for what you want to achieve with the change, the better prepared you will be for any 'unpredictable' surprises that will inevitably arise.

As I mentioned earlier in this book, one organisation I worked for started to renovate their office floors one by one. When it was my floor's turn to move, it was a very well-organised exercise that was well-led by the change managers involved.

The key objective of us moving to a more open plan space was to get us to collaborate more effectively and efficiently. There was therefore a distinct difference between the floor we were on (as project people) and the floor the legal teams were on.

The needs of the legal team were very different from the project teams, which require more collaboration space and less desk space.

While there was some adjusting, the open plan space and the collaboration spaces encouraged collaborative activity and people started taking the initiative to use those spaces more often. However, this would not have happened if people weren't clear about the objective for the move and how to use the space to their advantage. It was the repeated messages around collaboration and how to use the space effectively that helped people transition to the new way of working.

## 3. COMMUNICATE EARLY

A key mistake when leading change is that communication about a new technology solution starts too late and misses the opportunity for the wider organisation to get involved and buy in to the new solution, as I discussed in the introduction of this chapter.

Early engagement and communication to the wider organisation are critical to early adoption of the changes being introduced, and they also help reduce implementation risk and business disruption once the technology solution is launched. There is a difference between leadership when an organisation is in a time of peace versus leadership during a state of flux. These two different states require very different leadership skills to maintain momentum and ensure business results are achieved.

When an organisation is at peace, transactional leadership is required. This style of leadership is based on setting goals together with staff, setting tasks and providing rewards to staff based on their performance. Staff agree to follow the direction provided by the leader and work towards achieving their pre-set goals. Transactional leaders often focus on completing tasks as well as reviewing business performance results and taking action accordingly.

When an organisation is in a state of flux, however, transformational leadership is required. Transformational leadership depends on high levels of communication, motivation of staff and increasing productivity through communication and the high visibility of leaders. Transformational leaders focus their efforts on the bigger picture and delegate tasks as much as possible.[10]

A large-scale technology change puts your organisation in a state of flux, so transformational leadership is necessary. This involves communicating early, communicating transparently and communicating often.

You don't have to have all the answers before you start communicating the direction you want the business to go in. It is okay to communicate and share the areas where things haven't fully been worked out yet, as long as you also share the vision that underpins the change as well. The earlier you communicate, the less chance there is of conflicting messages travelling through the organisation and potentially reducing productivity. Through early

---

10   David Ingram, Demand Media, "Transformational Leadership Vs. Transactional Leadership", Chron

communication you will also get a higher level of participation and support for the change. People will feel included as they start to understand where the business wants to go. Lastly, early communication will also help with gathering diverse viewpoints and potentially valuable insights that can help enable the change and prevent potential roadblocks.

## 4. COMMUNICATE TRANSPARENTLY

Transparency is also essential. This involves sharing what you know about what is happening and where things are headed, but also what you don't know.

When you share what you know early on and let staff ask questions, they are not simply going to do as they are told, but they are going to think more deeply about what this means for their part of the business.

Removing the barriers of secrecy and mystery makes it easier for people to trust their leaders and their peers and it is much easier to offer assistance, suggestions and start thinking of new ways to help.

As a leader, transparent communication to build trust should be one of your main priorities. It will mobilise your employees to go above and beyond what is expected of them and it will ensure that those high-calibre people, those people you really need to have on your team to be successful, will stick around and will want to help you succeed.

Transparent communication involves giving regular updates, sharing the reasoning behind project priorities and changes, answering the difficult questions honestly and sharing business failings and mistakes.

You can also share some of your self-reflections. People can sense when you are trying too hard to be someone you are not. Show people that you are human, you have insecurities, you don't necessarily know everything, you have emotions and you experience stress just like they do. Admit you don't get it right every time, be aware of where you have dropped the ball and share that with your team (maybe for a bit of a laugh, even). People will be able to trust a leader who doesn't always need to have control over everything, a leader who is not afraid to show their weaknesses, a leader who is human! The more you can be your true self in front of one person as well as a group of hundreds of people, the more you will grow to be an authentic leader who feels comfortable and confident in the role.

## 5. COMMUNICATE OFTEN

The third key to communicating as a transformational leader is communicating often. Another common mistake I have seen in my experience of technology implementations is the lack of visibility of a leader throughout the implementation.

Yes, there are many priorities and many places a leader must be at any point in time. However, during transformational change the visibility of a leader sharing a clear message about the end goal is crucial. With regular communication, the leader can motivate staff and keep everyone involved focused on the end goal. Being visible strengthens the message, provides staff with a sense of belonging and gives them something to aspire to.

This links to the concepts 'leading by example' and 'walking the walk and talking the talk'. Let's take the example of a parent trying to educate their child on healthy eating habits. The parent writes a note that describes healthy eating habits, such as eating a variety of food, not skipping meals and eating at the dinner table. Yet the parent, due to a very demanding career, is hardly ever home to enjoy dinner with the child. The child hardly ever sees their parent practicing what they preach.

Do you think this child feels committed to healthy eating? Does the child feel a sense of belonging and wanting to follow the example that their parent has described to them? No. The child will probably simply eat whatever is on hand, whenever suits them, in front of the television.

Adults are not that different from children when it comes to how we learn and how we achieve our best. We achieve our best when we feel respected, we are in a safe environment and we have a secure sense of belonging. If you aren't a visible leader, it is likely your staff will feel neglected and lose their sense of belonging. They will forget where they are heading, they will feel like no one cares about the quality of their work, and they will lose momentum.

By contrast, you would be surprised by how motivated people will become if they regularly hear from you in some sort of personal dialogue and, more importantly, if they see you often. Hearing you speak about what you think is important, particularly hearing from you about your main concerns and how you would like to see the organisation overcome those concerns or risks and achieve its objectives. As a leader of change, this should be one of your highest priorities.

## 6. BE CONSCIOUS OF YOUR BODY LANGUAGE

### *Clare Mann, Psychologist, Trainer and Communications Expert - Communicate31, says:*

*"In order to lead, we must be aware of how our unconscious counter-intentions undermine our conscious ones. We can take steps to make conscious those unconscious drivers so they don't sabotage our efforts."*

In my career as a change manager I have found that body language is a very important aspect of being successful at collaborating with people.Your body language reveals a lot about your real intentions and, if you are not genuinely interested in what a person has to say, this will be revealed in your body language.

As a busy leader with a million things on your mind, it is sometimes very challenging to make time for individuals who ask you a question or to show your sincere interest in their challenges. In the bigger scheme of things, it may seem irrelevant.

However, this is an important part of being a leader. If you do not appear to be interested, this can be detrimental to collaboration and transformation success.

How can you appear interested? Besides setting the intention of being genuinely interested in what others have to say, there are six practical ways you can adjust your body language to appear interested and build a rapport.[11]

1.  **Ignore distractions:** If you focus on the person talking and ignore any other sounds or stimuli in the environment, the person will feel flattered by your level of interest.

2.  **Be still**: Moving around often indicates that someone is restless, distracted and/or disinterested. If you can be still while you listen to a person, it will help you focus on the dialogue.

3.  **Lean forward**: Physically moving towards the person speaking indicates that you are genuinely listening and focused on them.

4.  **Tilt your head**: A slightly tilted head indicates that you are curious. Exposing more of your neck will also show vulnerability and indicates you are comfortably listening to the person.

---

11   Changing Minds.org, "Attentive Body Language"

5.  **Steady your gaze**: An attentive listener looks at the person speaking without blinking too often or looking away. Gazing at the person speaking can also help prevent other stimuli from distracting you.

6.  **Furrow your brow**: If you are concentrating on what the person has to say, you can show this by bringing your eyebrows together. This can be helpful if there is a distance between you and the speaker or if there are background noises that you are trying to ignore while concentrating on the speaker.

As a leader it is important to be in the moment when you take the time to speak to people in the organisation.

Make yourself available regularly, so people know when they will have the opportunity to speak to you rather than interrupting you at times that are less convenient for you.

## 7. SHARE THE 'WHY' BEHIND YOUR VISION

Change is challenging. The strain that is put on employees during transformational change is incredible, and this is where resistance stems from. However, I've found people more easily adopt changes if they understand why the change is happening.

For employees in large organisations, the complaints I often come across include, 'I have no idea why we are doing this', 'Why do I have to continue doing these workarounds when they are spending all this money over there to increase efficiency?' and 'Why would they invest in that system and not in this system?'

If you have children, you would be familiar with telling them to do something only to have them ask you why. You answer by saying, 'Because I said so', but then they get frustrated, angry and start to complain. The end result is that they don't do a good job at what you asked them to do. The truth is that they are still resisting it because they don't know why it was so important, or why it was so important for you.

If a close friend called you and asked to borrow a substantial amount of money, how would you respond? 'Why do you need to borrow that kind of money? What do you need the money for?' If your friend answered by saying, 'Just trust me mate; you know I'll pay you back as soon as I can.'

You would be torn between wanting to help your friend, yet not wanting to lend the money without knowing exactly what it was for. You might think that, if you knew more about the problem, you could do something more constructive for your friend rather than just lending some money.

Not understanding the importance of the changes that are being made leaves staff feeling powerless. People need reasons for making changes. They need to feel that they can add value to the bigger picture. Giving them these reasons makes them more productive and happier in their roles.

When people understand the 'why' they will feel included and more motivated to make change happen. This communication is a critical responsibility of the leader to keep up the spirit in the workforce and ensure that people feel appreciated.

Some questions you could ask yourself are:

- Why do we need this technology innovation now and not next year, in two years or even in five years?

- Why are we focusing on investing our money in technology innovation when we are trying to reduce cost in other parts of the business?

- Why do we specifically need this type of technology innovation and not improvements to existing business process-es or technology solutions?

These are questions that would be going through people's heads and, if you provide clarity around these aspects, they have less reason to resist.

## 8. DEVELOP A COMMUNICATIONS PLAN

Open, transparent and frequent communication is the way to go, but how do you go about it? Who should you talk to and when? This is where a communications plan is valuable.

As with all communications, they have to be tailored to the audience in order to ensure it is relevant to the recipients. In Step 1 you started to identify your stakeholders. Now you need to understand how the individual stakeholders or groups of stakeholders will be impacted by the change. This insight will enable you to tailor your messages to be relevant to your audience.

Stakeholders who are the most impacted by the changes you are initiating should be the first to be engaged and get an understanding of your vision.

You can easily bring them up to speed on what the technology will bring to the organisation, as you have the documentation from Steps 1 and 2 to support your conversations. You will also be able to easily articulate how this technology will support the strategy of the organisation in the coming years, as you have the vision clearly articulated.

In order for you to be organised and efficient with your time as well as sharing new messages at the right time to the right audience, you need a robust stakeholder engagement and communication plan. This plan will help you communicate to the right stakeholders at the right time with the right information. A stakeholder engagement and communications plan should include:

- A list of each individual stakeholder (or stakeholder group).
- The types of communication channels that you can use to reach your audience,

such as one-to-one meetings, town halls, newsletters, lunch and learn sessions, intranet and email.

- The frequency of communication to each stakeholder (per communication channel).

- A high-level description of how the change impacts the stakeholder.

- A high-level description of the message you want to convey based on the audience and impacts related to each stakeholder (or stakeholder group).

- A detailed communication schedule, including the different communication channels you will use to repeat the same message (not limiting your communication to only verbal or email communication).

Something to keep in mind is the importance of face-to-face communication in conjunction with regular email updates or other verbal communications. The communication method you choose can make the difference between effective communication that brings people together and complete resistance.

Also repeating the same message via different communication channels is crucial, as research shows that a message has to be repeated several times to be effective.

Unlike face-to-face communication or video-conferences, the lack of nonverbal cues in email – such as body language, volume, pitch and speed – mean not all information can be fully transferred.[12] As a result, it is difficult to interpret the emotions of the sender and to convey your own emotions, as most nonverbal communication happens subconsciously. I am sure there are many examples that you can think of where an email has been interpreted incorrectly and has consequently required additional clarification.

While email is a very easy way to feel like you are in frequent communication with your staff and the business, once it is over-used it could be detrimental to your goals. Consider connecting with a friend in another city or country via email, phone and social media. How would you feel if your friend visited your city without reaching out to connect face-to-face? I would be terribly disappointed and feel that the value of this relationship had diminished as the friend or relative did not think it is important to meet with me in person.

This holds true for staff in large organisations. When a leader fails to ever make a face-to-face connection, staff will start to feel neglected. Emails or other forms of verbal communication start to mean less as it feels like the leader doesn't care that much anyway. Once staff start to feel this way, it is a very hard to turn them around. This feeling of neglect can develop into plain resistance and will achieve the opposite of productivity and transformation..For this reason, there needs to be a good balance between face-to-face communication and nonverbal communication in your communication plan.

12   Derks, D., & Bakker, A., "The Impact of E-mail Communication on Organizational Life", Cyberpsychology, *Journal of Psychosocial Research on Cyberspace*, 4(1), article 1, McKenna & Bargh, 2000

Your communication plan will provide you and your assistant with an easy-to-follow schedule of one-off or periodic one-on-one meetings or attendance to existing forums to share your vision and knowledge of the technology innovation. Once your peers and direct reports are fully across this, you can also ask them to take it further into the organisation as well.

While you communicate to your stakeholders it is important to identify those people that can be advocates for the technology innovation and can assist you with the transformation.

Try to mobilise these change advocates in such a way that they understand how they can help you and play an active role implementing the changes across the organisation.

Incorporate the communication activities of your change advocates in your overall communications plan and meet with them on a regular basis in order to ensure that all parts of the organisation will be provided with relevant and equally important, consistent information during the course of the implementation.

Having this plan in place will give you comfort that you are well organised, prepared and will speak to the right people at the right time with the right message.

## COLLABORATING WITH YOUR TEAM

Albert Einstein once said, *'The difference between stupidity and genius is that genius has its limits.'*

This quote sums up the strength of delegating wisely. As a leader, you cannot do it alone. With your busy schedule, many priorities and the overwhelming amount of information you have to get through on a daily basis, adding technology transformation to the equation is unrealistic. You need a team to succeed.

By working with a team, you will be able to fill your knowledge gaps and be empowered to make the best decisions for the business as a whole. As a leader you simply cannot know everything. You have the capacity to see the bigger picture and make the difficult decisions and you have your own areas of expertise. However, there are often smaller issues you won't be aware of, so surround yourself with trusted advisers regarding these areas.

Realise that, as a leader, you have the ability to really make significant and extraordinary things happen simply by making people your priority rather than information gathering. The people around you will manage each bit of information. Your role is to empower them. Following are six tips on successfully building and collaborating with your project team.

## 1. CHOOSE THE RIGHT RESOURCES

The type of professionals you want to hire are people who have experience with technology implementations, a great understanding of both technology and technology language, as well as a good understanding of business and business processes. They need to be able to translate this understanding and these insights into different types of communication to make them accessible to others in the business.

These professionals may include:

- **Project manager**: This is likely one of the first roles you would look for and it is a pivotal role. The key is to find someone who not only has significant experience in implementing complex technology systems effectively into the business (preferably with experience in financial services), but who is a good cultural fit. Project managers need to portray the of leadership that best suits your organisation, as that will be the most effective with the high-calibre people you have in your organisation. In some ways the project manager should embody some of the traits I discussed earlier in this chapter and demonstrate an open, transparent and authentic leadership style in order to bring the best out of the project team as well as the key stakeholders in the business. So do not blindly go with the project manager who is the most experienced in the field – it is equally, if not more, important to have a suitable leader who can manage people, budgets and tight timeframes effectively and successfully.

- **Change manager**: This role is fairly difficult to define as there are many aspects to the change management role that are misunderstood. Change managers should be able to follow a methodology or structured approach in order to identify the stakeholders affected by the change, manage the impacts and provide a comprehensive implementation plan in order to help everyone involved accept the changes. However, in my experience the most important aspect to this role is being a trusted adviser. Change managers have the opportunity to collaborate closely with all levels of the organisation and gain incredible insight into what prohibits people from adopting changes. This can be a very valuable resource for you as a leader to gain more in depth knowledge about the people in your organisation and their challenges.

- **Business implementation manager**: Similar to the change manager, this role assists the business with implementing the changes that are required in order to successfully adopt the new technology. There are a lot of similarities with the change manager role and maybe even some overlaps with the project manager role, but the significant difference is that this role will work with the business to look at optimising their business processes in order to more effectively adopt and use the new technology. This can be very important if you don't just want to implement the technology, but are also looking to optimise business processes and business outcomes.

- **Technology architect:** Rather than a single role, there will usually be a team of technology experts working with the architect to find ways of integrating the new technology most effectively in the existing technology landscape. A key requirement here is for someone who can be a conduit between the business and the technology department. The architect needs to understand the business challenges intimately and be able to apply this knowledge to a highly complex technology landscape with its own challenges. It is important for the successful implementation of your technology that your architect understands the importance of the business requirements. The aim is to improve the business, not to create the most high-tech solution in the shortest amount of time for the lowest budget, so look for an architect with a drive for business innovation and improvement and not just a high level of expertise in your technology landscape.

- **Business analyst:** Technology implementations require a significant amount of requirements gathering, which can be challenging considering the requirements are defined from a business perspective and have to be translated into technology speak. A technology implementation can also come with a large amount of process re-engineering, a capability that is often overlooked. There are great business analysts out there who are very good at mapping out existing as well as new business processes in order to define what the change will be for the business in more detail.

It is likely you will need several business analysts with a blend of skills, including the skill to collect business requirements and translate them into technology requirements, and the skill to map out existing business processes and understand as well as define what the new business processes should look like once the technology solution is in place.

- **Subject-matter experts:** The role of the subject-matter expert is not to be underestimated. Most likely you will need experts from a few different areas, including the technology solution, the business areas that will be impacted by the change and also the existing technology landscape. Some of these roles are best filled by people within the organisation, but you will also need to complement them with expert advice from outside the organisation.

## 2. RECRUIT DIVERSITY

In our day-to-day life it is easy to surround ourselves with likeminded people. It is the same as when you were a child and you wanted to fit in at school. You would make sure you dressed in the same way as the other children, that your hairstyle was in line with the latest trends and that you were talking about the type of subjects your school mates would want to talk about.

However, society is starting to embrace diversity, and for good reason too. In business, diversity will help you and your team be creative thinkers and develop new ways to improve efficiency, customer service and, in the end, the bottom line.

This will create new solutions to existing problems.

When building your team, consider pulling together the most diverse people in your organisation, who will challenge each other's thinking and come up with new, creative solutions.

## 3. FOCUS ON THE BIGGER PICTURE

Do you often feel like you can't add any value to the technology implementation as the experts, the 'techos', have got it in hand? Do you feel like you don't understand enough about the complexities of the technology to add meaningful value? Do you think that, while the implementation is underway, it is better not to distract them and interfere with the project?

I think nothing is further from the truth. The role of these experts is to focus on the areas in which they have expertise. However, this focus often means that the overarching vision and business objectives are lost (or, at the very least, out of sight). Due to time pressures, budget constraints and conflicting priorities, ensuring the solution is still aligned with the core business objectives is a challenge. What was most important to the business could easily be the first thing that is dropped from the scope, as it becomes too hard from a technology perspective or it risks delay and pushing the project over budget.

Your role as the leader is to focus on the bigger picture and the end goal for the transformation, and keeping your team on track through the pressures, constraints and challenges that come their way. Because you have this broader perspective, you have the ability to assess the challenges against what will benefit the organisation most. You can then make the final decision on whether to address these challenges or simply let go of certain aspects of the technology solution.

It is not about studying the detail behind every moving part of the business you are responsible for. You have not risen to the top of the ladder to be diving into detailed design documents – leave that to your team of professionals. You need very little information to understand the initiative, change or circumstance you have to deal with. Your focus is to tie all those pieces together and make sense of the bigger picture.

## 4. SHARING YOUR PRIORITIES

Once you have a reasonably sized team of professionals on the project as well as leaders from around the organisation (who can be your change advocates), you will discover that each person will have a specific role to play in making the change happen. In order to do this, you need to provide them with insight into the bigger picture and share the big-ticket items you are focused on.

Even though a leader in your team might not be directly impacted by some changes you are introducing, they might still be able to offer assistance or ideas. It could be that members of your team have been in different parts of the business previously, or other organisations that introduced a similar change, or they may have had experience with the technology you are investing in.

By ensuring there is transparency about your business priorities, you provide your team with clarity on what is happening and empower them to assist where they can while meeting their own objectives.

Sharing your priorities and having your team members share their priorities ensures everyone is on the same page and focused on the right things.

In addition to sharing the priorities themselves, it is important to make sure the reasoning behind these priorities is understood.

As I discussed when it came to communicating with the wider business, providing people with an understanding of why different items are key priorities will make them feel included and it will help them accept and understand why other business issues are not a top priority right now.

The bottom line is that open, honest and transparent communication by you, the leader, is crucial to the success of technology driven transformation.

## 5. INVOLVE YOUR TEAM IN YOUR VISION

In the Forbes article, *8 Tips For Collaborative Leadership*, body language expert Carol Kinsey Goman states, 'The power of a vision comes truly into play only when the employees themselves have had some part in its creation.'[13]

You as a leader play a critical role in making sure the team around you understands as much of the challenges that the organisation faces as well as the strategic direction of the organisation. These factors are all relevant for people downstream, as they help them understand why their business ideas or pain points may not be addressed right now and why other investments are occurring.

If people are left in the dark about the reasons behind certain changes, they feel they are not part of the solution, they are not important and they lose their sense of belonging. These negative feelings will cause a loss of productivity and creativity in the workforce, which can be disastrous for your business. You can easily reduce this risk or even eliminate it if you are articulate and transparent about your

---

13 Carol Kinsey Goman, "8 Tips For Collaborative Leadership", Forbes, 13 February 2014

key priorities and why they are your priorities. You can also go a step further and show empathy to these people about the challenges they face day-to-day and that you realise the need for other improvements and investments across the organisation.

You can share the limitations of the organisation as well as the fact that you need to focus first on the things that are in line with the strategy, best serve the needs of the customer and are currently the biggest strain on the organisation's bottom line.

The vision of the organisation should not just be owned by senior leadership, but should be owned and adopted by all people in the organisation.

That is when it is most effective. People will feel included and have a sense of belonging when they understand where the organisation is headed and why.

## 6. HELP TEAM MEMBERS DEVELOP RELATIONSHIPS

The power of personal connections in the workplace is under-researched and under-appreciated by leaders.

Many leaders barely make it to their monthly stand-ups, let alone make an effort to organise social encounters between employees.

However, as a leader you can, and should, provide your employees with the opportunity and environment to connect with their (new) team members and create relationships, as well as create a common understanding of the project or business objective they are going to be working on.

It is easy to see that working with people you see eye-to-eye with is much easier than working with someone you dislike. People will work that little bit harder for the colleagues they have an established relationship with and a level of common understanding with.

Teams work more effectively and efficiently together if they have had a bit of time to connect and find some common ground. This makes team lunches, afternoon beverages and team events worthy investments.

## KEY TAKEAWAYS

1. Having a stakeholder engagement and communication plans in place will make you feel confident that you will engage and communicate to the right people at the right time with the right information.

2. Choose a diverse team of the right professionals to help you deliver your vision and ensure that they feel empowered to make decisions as well as work effectively as a team.

3. Communicating openly about your vision, sharing your key priorities with your team and being transparent about what you do and what you don't know will show that you are human and make you an authentic and trustworthy leader of change.

# Step 4: **Control**

*'Intellectuals solve problems, geniuses prevent them.'*

*— Albert Einstein*

Risk management is not always top of mind when projects are focused on tight timelines, complex technology requirements, managing budgets and managing resources to deliver quality outcomes.

Knowing potential risks will help you not only to manage these risks in preparation for the launch of the new technology, it will greatly assist in keeping the project running within the set timeframes and on budget, as managing risks early means there is time to plan the mitigation activities and fit them into the schedule.

The earlier risks can be raised, the better they can be managed and prevented from becoming issues that result in business disruption.

Yet some change leaders resist the idea of risk management, arguing that it's the project team's responsibility. My belief is that, as a leader of change, *you* should play a significant role in looking at the bigger picture from a risk management perspective, as you are the one who is best placed to understand what external and internal changes may potentially influence the technology implementation and business continuity.

How can you do this? The first step is recognising your role in the risk management process, after which you and your team will follow a process of ongoing risk identification and management.

# YOUR ROLE IN THE RISK MANAGEMENT PROCESS

Risk management on large, technology innovation programs is a fairly common practice in large corporations these days. Generally, a risk partner is assigned to help facilitate brainstorming sessions with the project team to define project risks up front. Throughout the project, they will revisit those risks identified in order to ensure they are being mitigated.

However, the people involved in these brainstorm sessions are often limited in their knowledge of the potential risks. The project team is focusing on the day-to-day challenges of translating business requirements into technical requirements and designing and implementing a solution, which means they can lose sight of the overall picture. Meanwhile, those representing a particular part of the business that is involved with the project will be focused on impacts to their part of the business. As a result, the view of the broader organisation or even the external market place is not represented in this risk assessment and certain business and project impacts are therefore more likely to be missed.

It is therefore important that you as a leader can assess the critical project decisions against the bigger organisational and industry picture.

Large enterprise-wide technology innovation programs can run for years. Over that time, many changes take place across in the broader organisation and in the marketplace.

Specifically in the financial services industry, legislative changes have come through rapidly in recent years with the Future of Financial Advice reforms being introduced in July 2012, while digitalisation and changes in consumer demands are driving large corporations to change their strategies and focus on innovation.

While investments in large-scale technology innovations are often aligned with some of these changes in the marketplace, the requirements of these innovations can change over time due to new changes in the legislation, consumer demands or the competition.

While some change leaders argue that risk management is the project team's responsibility, the project team, unfortunately, doesn't have visibility of these changes. This not only means that risks related to changes in the broader organisation or in the marketplace are not being identified or managed, this also means that decisions the project team makes are based on incomplete information and this could be detrimental to the business outcome of the project.

As a leader, you have a much clearer view of what lies ahead and what direction the business is taking than members of the project team.

If changes in the marketplace or in the broader organisation mean the direction of the project has to be changed, you would have to agree that it is better to make this change as soon as this information arises rather than waiting until the project delivers and the outcome does not meet the most current business needs and objectives. A decision to change the strategy of a large-scale technology innovation project is not an easy one, but making this decision as soon as information is available means that significant rework, business disruption and disappointment can potentially be prevented. The cost of simply not taking any action based on significant changes in the broader business landscape would be a lot higher.

Ultimately, the benefits of this oversight are two-fold. First, you can better determine if the project's efforts (such as mitigating certain risks) are focused on the right things. Second, better informed decisions can be made by the project, which could otherwise result in wasted effort, loss of funding or a technology solution that does not match the business's potentially changed strategy and vision.

Your role as a change leader is to guide the project team in the right direction and ensure that, despite all internal and external factors, business continuity is guaranteed. Being involved in risk management is a part of that role.

# RISK IDENTIFICATION

Once you accept your role in the risk management process, the first step of that process is risk identification. In order to ensure we align our thinking about what risks are, I reiterate what I mean here with risks. Risks are those events that have the potential to occur and cause a detrimental impact on customers, employees, shareholders, as well as processes, systems and business financials. Risks can become issues if the potential event has actually taken place and an issue or (in some businesses referred to as) significant event has occurred. In this book we are not addressing issues, we are talking about the identification and mitigation of risks only.

In other words, risks need to be identified and managed in order to prevent negative events from occurring that could have a detrimental impact on the organisation and your technology innovation project.Project teams generally assess the risks related to the project based on the following aspects:

- Delivery timeline.
- Project budget.
- Business continuity.
- Business benefit realisation.

Considering all these aspects are defined up front and are generally left unchanged, unless there is a formal request to make a change during the project, the risks identified in association with these aspects are relatively stagnant.

However, the market place, technology innovation and other business related change is happening at a faster pace than ever before. In projects that can run for years, these changes will have a significant impact on the desired outcome of the technology innovation project. As a result, the broader oversight that you bring to the risk identification process will include a very different set of potential risks. Risks that should be considered, but that generally are not incorporated in a project risk assessment, include:

- **Operational efficiency risks, such as:**

  o Skilled and motivated people leaving the organisation due to increased stress levels during times of change and the lack of improvement in the workplace (including business process improvement, technology innovation, and the company culture).

  o Lack of optimisation of business processes due to the focus being on the technology aspects of the innovation and the technical feasibility of the innovation, rather than the business benefits. Also, silos can create a lack of business process optimisation or even duplication of business processes due to a lack of transparent communication between business divisions.

  o Loss of staff productivity due to staff not being informed and prepared for change when it happens, or even due to unplanned system downtime.

  o Unmanaged business change programs (other than your technology innovation program). If change is managed poorly in other parts of the business, this can have a detrimental impact on your technology innovation project. There will likely be a crossover of stakeholders and impacted staff, who will be left frustrated, stressed and unproductive due to the impact of other changes in the business that were not well managed.

- **Return on investment risks, such as:**

  o The lack of optimisation of business process costs due to too great a focus on the technical feasibility and the project budget and timeline rather than the business benefits.

  o Lack of optimisation of product and service costs (cause is as per the above 'optimisation of business process costs').

  o Loss of continued investment from shareholders due to the lack of trust in the ability of the organisation to stay on top of their innovation agenda as well as growing the business.

- **Competitive advantage risks, such as:**

  o Lack of organisational agility to respond to changes in the marketplace and the need for business and technology innovation at a reasonably fast pace. This can relate to the culture of the organisation as well as the way change is led and managed.

o Loss of product and service demand due to business disruption caused by changes in the organisation that were not well planned and/or managed.

o Lack of customer-oriented service culture, causing the technology innovation project to not achieve its full potential to improve service to the customer and increase the company's bottom line.

o Lack of innovation due to a lack of vision and expertise within the organisation to lead business and technology innovation projects and create real business benefits.

• **Reducing the overall company risk profile, such as:**

o Compliance with internal policies.

o Compliance with laws and regulations.

o Business resiliency, such as business continuity plans.

o Strategic risk-based decision making.

# REVISITING RISK

Many projects do a risk management workshop early on in the project never to repeat the exercise. However, when the project is further along and more knowledge is gained, it's not unusual for some risks to be mitigated and for new ones to come out of the woodwork.

When these risks arise and the project comes across a roadblock (these are often in relation to the implementation of the technology solution, the project timeline and/or the project budget), the project team tends to over analyse potential solutions from a technology perspective and while under analysing the business risks associated with the roadblock (if they are analysed at all). Often, roadblocks result in technology solutions being proposed and implemented to keep the project going, but result in less business functionality and improvement.

This is where it's crucial for you to step in as the leader of change. With most technology transformations taking over a number of years, risk identification is ongoing due to the constantly changing external environment and internal environments. Therefore, your involvement in risk management goes much further than just performing an initial risk assessment on the project itself.

Your role is to ensure that appropriate governance is applied, sufficient evidence is gathered and that decisions are made by the right people, with the right level of authority and with the right level of oversight. It's only then that the project will maintain alignment with the overarching business strategy and vision.

For this reason I believe risks should be discussed at each and every status and team meeting. This includes the meetings you have with your direct reports, your peers as well as with the project team.

As a leader, your ability to continue to ask questions about how developments across the organisation will impact the technology transformation will make sure that people proactively consider the consequences for the technology innovation.

For example, if there is an update on legislative changes, immediately ask your team how these legislative changes might affect the transformation project. If there are other business or technology transformations underway in other parts of the business, make sure there are regular conversations between the different initiatives in order to manage potential overlaps, integration opportunities and potential risks. This creates an interactive, collaborative environment where people are responsible and accountable for identifying risks and raising them for proactive mitigation.

The outcome of this interactive and ongoing risk identification process is two-fold:

- People will feel empowered by the fact that their leader wants to learn from them, which will motivate them to be more proactive about the identification of risks that might impact the success of the transformation.

- People will feel a sense of responsibility. As the leader is asking *them* about potential impacts of business changes, this might mean someone else doesn't know or has not identified any impacts. This will create a broader sense of responsibility and accountability for the changes happening in the organisation. It is also a great way to create a more collaborative and inclusive work environment.

# MANAGING RISKS

The risk management process can be managed or coordinated by the project team, but should not be limited to the project team's involvement. Business involvement is paramount when managing risk.

Risks are generally managed by the responsible project team through:

1. **Assessment of the likelihood of the risk occurring.** Risks identified can have a higher or lower level of likelihood of occurring. Also once mitigation plans are in place, this likelihood can lower.

   To ensure the focus is on the most urgent and most important risks, this likelihood rating can help with prioritising the risks and focussing on those risks that have the highest likelihood of becoming an issue.

2. **Assessment of the level of impact the risk would have on the organisation if it occurred.** There are different types of

impacts risks can have on an organisation and some are more damaging to business continuity than others. This assessment is to determine if the risk can cause monetary, reputational or legal impacts for the organisation.

3. **Prioritisation of the risks based on business impact (type and severity) and likelihood.** Based on the likelihood of the risk occurring and the severity (and type) of the impact it would have on the organisation, the risks can be prioritised to ensure the more urgent and higher impact risks get immediate attention.

4. **Establishing a mitigation strategy**. Once risks have been identified and prioritised based on impact levels and likelihood, a mitigation strategy and plan needs to be agreed with relevant stakeholders in the business to reduce the likelihood of the risk eventuating, or to eliminate the risk all together. These mitigation strategies should include a clear step-by-step action plan and an agreed timeframe.

5. **Monitoring the implementation of the mitigation strategy**. The mitigation strategy should be monitored to ensure that it will eliminate the likelihood of the risk event occurring or will even eliminate the risk completely. This involves assigning a responsible individual ('the owner') to each

risk in order to oversee the risk mitigation plans being executed as agreed and within the agreed timeframes.

6.  **Regular reporting to senior management.** I believe managing risks is about open and transparent communication around the risks on a regular basis. In order to do this, I recommend detailed recording of risks at the project level along with an executive summary of the high-priority risks that require awareness by senior management. The correct information can then also be shared with the broader organisation.

When it comes to sharing this information with the broader organisation, the key is to be concise and to the point when reporting on risk. Considering the project team works in the detail, this can be a significant challenge. As much as you don't want to bother the project team with seemingly minor issues such as concise and specific reporting of risks (as well as other status updates), I urge you coach the project team members to improve their communication by cutting out the unnecessary detail. Unnecessary detail can cause important information to get lost, important questions to be left unasked and the key causes of the risks remaining unaddressed. Therefore, concise communication about risks is as important as ensuring that these risks are shared with the organisation in the first place and the agreed mitigation strategies are in place.

# RISK MANAGEMENT LEARNINGS FROM INTEL IT

Finally, I would like to share some further learnings from Intel IT. In the introduction I mentioned a 2013 white paper published by Intel titled *Aligning IT with Business Goals through Strategic Planning*.[14] This white paper shared the company's new approach to strategic planning, including valuable advice for managing the risks of projects with a high number of interdependencies.

These learnings included:

- **Defining the integration points to the governance processes:** Ensure that your project governance has integration points with both IT and the strategic direction of the organisation. It is often the lack of oversight across both IT and the business that drives bad decision making.

- **Defining and managing planning data:** Defining the parameters against which you are going to measure the project will prevent wasted time and confusing messages. It will also ensure there is a consistent way to measure progress and success.

- **Defining and publicising the planning calendar:** There are always many different

---

14   Intel Corporation, "Aligning IT with Business Goals through Strategic Planning", *Whitepaper Intel Information Technology, December 2008*

activities happening around large organisations – transformational, project-driven and business-as-usual activities. Agreeing set times to publicise the activities and milestones that are current and in the pipeline will provide all people involved with the clarity they need to focus on the right things at the right time. It will also help them plan around activities and constraints that may impact other parts of the business.

- **Realising that timing is essential:** When multiple changes and even multiple large-scale technology implementations are happening at the same time, timing is everything. Planning and decision-making needs to occur at the right time and needs to happen in close collaboration with all relevant leaders and expert parties to ensure full visibility of the scale of the changes happening across the organisation.

- **Clearly defining roles and responsibilities:** Clarity around roles and responsibilities is important in any business, but it becomes increasingly important during the implementation of a significant change. It is essential the people you have gathered to drive and implement the technology solution have a very clear understanding of what their roles and responsibilities are. This will increase the level of accountability and ensure nothing can fall through the cracks. It is also easy to identify who to consult with regarding different parts of the transformation, and for other parts of the business to know who to contact if they have specific questions about aspects of the technology or changes that are occurring.

- **Communicating data and messages well:** As the white paper stated, 'Well-informed employees are most likely to commit to and support the plan.' This is very much in line with what I've discussed in the earlier steps in this book – open and transparent communication is paramount to create buy-in from all people involved in the change.

These learnings from Intel IT highlight the need to communicate and collaborate closely with the broader organisation in order to effectively manage overlaps in scope, timing of delivery as well as other business risks for your transformation project.

## *KEY TAKEAWAYS*

1. The identification of risks should be an ongoing part of everyday operations due to the rapid pace of change in and around organisations. Incorporate the topic of risk management into most, if not all, of your meetings.

2. As a change leader, having clear oversight of the risks associated with your transformation projects, changes in other parts of the business and external changes, will empower you to steer the project and the business in the right direction and give you the confidence you need to lead the changes well.

3. In order to enable the broader organisation to help manage and mitigate risks for your technology innovation project, ensure that the reporting of risks is open, transparent and, most importantly concise. This means that the communication of risk has to be in plain and easy-to-understand language, removing technology jargon and unnecessary complexities.

Conclusion:
# Become a great leader of change

*'Strive not to be a success, but to be of value.'*

*– Albert Einstein*

The financial services landscape is changing more rapidly than ever before, and there is no mercy for those who are not able to keep up.

Just some recent changes include changes to legislation to improve trust and confidence in the financial services industry, increased competition as more boutique financial service firms start tackling the larger corporations, and the fact that consumers are getting smarter and more demanding. Add to this the changes in human interaction due to ongoing developments in online communication and social media, and effective leadership is more challenging than ever.

All of this change requires us to reflect on how we as individuals perform among these volatilities and, specifically, how we *lead*.

The approach described in this book will help you manage these challenges and successfully lead technology innovations in your business.

In Step 1 you discovered the value of learning from organisations that have gone before you. Organisations that have already implemented the technology solution you are considering can provide insight into potential challenges as well as highlighting how you can get the most out of the new technology solution to meet your business objectives. This research will give you the clarity you need to make well informed decisions right from the start and provide you and your team with more certainty around expectations for the technology implementation.

In Step 2 I discussed the value of becoming clear on the key business drivers for the technology innovation by assessing the challenges raised by the broader business. You learned the importance of involving the broader organisation and how this information could be compiled in a clear vision and roadmap that would share *what* the technology solution would achieve, *why* the organisation needs to invest in the technology innovation and *when* the business benefits would be realised. Sharing this vision and roadmap early and with as many people as possible will then create increased certainty, early buy-in and a clear direction for all involved.

In Step 3 I explored the benefits of real collaboration, including the consideration of diverse views from across the business. As a change leader you should be collaborating with your peers, your leadership team, your project team and the broader organisation. You learned that, in order to do this, you need to be an open, transparent, authentic and visible communicator who creates an environment where all suggestions, thoughts, questions and comments are welcome. This will then create an increased level of certainty, lessen the impact of change on productivity and will make staff want to work harder towards common goals.

Finally, Step 4 focused on your role as a change leader in relation to managing risks. You learned about integrating the identification of risks in your day-to-day management of the business, as well as the need to consider not only the risks directly related to the project, such as budget, project timeframes and scope, but also the influence of changes that are happening elsewhere in the organisation and in the wider marketplace. Most of these risks will be unknown to the business, which requires proactive thinking about the consequences of the change by the entire organisation.

Now I'm handing the reins over to you.

I realise that there are leaders out there who have climbed up the ranks because they are exceptionally good at what they do – they have a wealth of knowledge and experience and a great track record for delivering great results. This may sound like your career path. The catch is that being a transformational leader requires far less of your functional skills and expertise and far more of your interpersonal skills.

It is no longer up to you to produce the outcomes. Technology driven change is not just about implementing a complex new system, it is about the people that make that system work to achieve the benefits for the organisation.

However, change is uncertain, leaving many of us feeling threatened or even lost. In an organisation, this uncertainty kills creativity, innovation and productivity, all of which are necessary for successful transformational change.

Consequently, if today's organisations don't focus more on the human aspect of technology driven change, they will continue to fail miserably when it comes to achieving its full potential.

As a leader, this means your role is to mobilise and empower people. This requires collaboration and being open to diverse views, new ways of thinking and different ways of resolving existing challenges, both within your immediate team and across the organisation as a whole.

On one hand, it's a little nerve-wracking. On the other, it's an exciting challenge! You have the opportunity to be a great leader of change. You have the opportunity to empower people to succeed in their professional lives and, through this, you have the opportunity to have a positive impact on their personal lives as well. You have the opportunity to not only lead business transformation, but to make it easier, more creative, more collaborative and even fun!

Change is not going anywhere, and as a senior leader you are instrumental in helping your organisation navigate it successfully. The more you make this your top priority, the more successful your business's technology implementations will be.

I hope this book will give you the tools to become more confident in your role as a leader, live a better life because of it and inspire others to do the same.

# Acknowledgements

A little over a year ago I received an email from my colleague and friend Christina Morgan-Meldrum with a link to attend the Key Person of Influence (KPI) Business Brand Accelerator. As with most things, I followed my gut and attended the event, which led to me writing my very own book!

So my first thank you goes out to Christina, as I would have never started this journey if it wasn't for you prompting me to give this a go and pursue my dream of having my own business one day.

Staying on the topic of KPI, a huge thank you should also go out to the very inspirational and wonderful Andrew Griffiths, who convinced me the very first time I heard him speak that I could write a book. Thank you Andrew for your incredible energy and drive to make us entrepreneurs the best people we can possibly be.

Thank you also to the broader KPI team, who are all amazing at what they do and have made this past year an extremely exhilarating and rewarding experience.

A very big call out goes to my wonderful 'GSD' accountability group, The Bransons. Thank you Paul O'Dwyer, Andrew Bycroft, Amanda Howe, Therese Tarlinton and Mark Coburn for your passion, commitment and support on my journey. I have grown to love and admire all of you and hope our friendship sees us all into a long and successful future.

In preparation for this book I approached a number of leaders in the financial services industry as well as other experts and I would like to express my gratitude for them offering their time for some open and frank discussions, even though in most cases I was a complete stranger who approached them via LinkedIn! I'd specifically like to thank Rod Finch, Sean O'Malley, James Kent, Paul Franks, John Henson, Paul Harrop, Brad Kane, Muneesh Wadhwa, Michael Neary, Erwin van der Koogh and Clare Mann. Thank you so much for sharing your expert leadership knowledge and advice with me. I have grown from every conversation.

Thank you to the lovely and hugely talented Julia Kuris for your patience in developing my book cover as well as my brand. I look forward to collaborating with you a lot more in the future as your passion and excitement throughout the development process is contagious.

The first person who ever read my book in its most raw form was the wonderful Janine Holgate. You have no idea how much it meant to me when you reviewed this book and how much confidence and drive you gave me to keep going and get this book published. I am very grateful to have met you and I thank you so very much for believing in me.

Thank you also to the incredibly talented Jacqui Pretty, my editor. Even though she cut a good thirteen thousand words out of my original manuscript, she blew me away with what she did to bring my book together and create the professional read I was after. You are incredible at what you do and I won't fail to mention that to anyone who wants to hear it.

Thank you Andrew Akratos for generously sharing your knowledge about what it takes to publish a book and your patience in answering all my rookie questions.

Thank you to the talented, calm and wonderful Dee Gerlach for making me look a million bucks on this cover and managing to do that while dealing with very challenging circumstances.

Thank you to Chris, my brother, for believing I can do anything, as well as my parents, for loving me unconditionally.

To my two beautiful daughters, Sienna and Ariella, who make me smile every day and make my heart well up every time I look at them. Ariella was still growing inside me as I started the journey of writing this book. You are both my inspiration to keep pushing forward on my dream and create the best possible future for our family. I truly feel blessed and honoured to be your mother and I will do my best to be the best possible role model for you both.

Last but not least, to my amazing, loving and truly selfless husband, Richard, who never ceases to believe in me, love me and support me. I often ask myself, 'How did I get so lucky?' You make me a better person, a better woman, a better wife and a better mother each day and I am so grateful for sharing my life with you and our beautiful girls. Thank you for your never-ending wisdom, patience, support and belief in me. This would not have been possible without you!

# About the author

Esther De La Cruz has a real passion for great leadership and for simplifying complex change. She has seen firsthand the power of great leadership during times of change. On the flip side, she has also experienced the challenges leaders face when managing large complex technology change and the effect these have on everyone involved.

With over fifteen years of change management experience, including several enterprise-wide technology innovation programs for blue chip organisations like Sterigenics, Valvoline, Qantas, NAB, Westpac and AMP, Esther has gained an incredible insight into how to help people adapt to change quickly and effectively. With the influence of great leadership, she has discovered that people can really flourish and excel during times of change.

To make work environments more adaptive to change, Esther believes that change leadership is paramount. Her mission is to help business leaders become better leaders of change through her four-step method for confidently leading technology driven change. By following this methodology, large corporations have the opportunity to be more efficient and effective when managing change, while also creating a healthier and happier work environment for their employees.

Esther also believes in sharing the knowledge we gain through western education and our working life with less fortunate societies, such as third world countries. If we can be more efficient in managing change in our society – saving money and time and, most importantly, creating a healthy work environment – we can share more of our resources and expertise with those who need them most.

Esther loves hearing from her readers
and can be reached on:


Twitter: EsthereDELACRUZ

LinkedIn: Estherdelacruz

Email: esther@leaderofchange.com.au

Website: www.leaderofchange.com.au

www.ingramcontent.com/pod-product-compliance
Lightning Source LLC
Chambersburg PA
CBHW062005200326
41519CB00017B/4675